# AN AWAKENED LIFE

# AN AWAKENED LIFE

*Uncommon Wisdom from Everyday Experience*

Christopher Titmuss

SHAMBHALA
*Boston*
2000

Shambhala Publications, Inc.
Horticultural Hall
300 Massachusetts Avenue
Boston, Massachusetts 02115
*www.shambhala.com*

9  8  7  6  5  4  3  2  1

First Shambhala edition

Printed in the United States of America

♾ This edition is printed on acid-free paper that meets the
American National Standards Institute Z39.48 Standard.
Distributed in the United Stated by Random House, Inc.,
and in Canada by Random House of Canada Ltd

Library of Congress Cataloging-in-Publication Data
Titmuss, Christopher.
An awakened life: uncommon wisdom from everyday experience /
Christopher Titmuss—1st ed.
p.  cm.
ISBN 1-57062-564-6 (paper)
1. Buddhism—Doctrines—Introductions. I. Title.
BQ4132.A576   2000
294.3'4—dc21
99-056765

# CONTENTS

# CONTENTS

## THE PRACTICE OF UNDERSTANDING

CONTENTS

## THE DISCOVERY OF LIBERATION

# Acknowledgements

I wish to express my deepest appreciation to the Buddha and his teachings on freedom for humanity. He unwaveringly kept to this focus throughout his life. I wish to express equal appreciation to Jesus of Nazareth for his profound message of love and liberation for all.

My gratitude also goes to the late Venerable Ajahn Buddhadasa and Venerable Ajahn Dhammadharo of Thailand, both of whom were immensely influential during my six years as a Buddhist monk.

The inspiration for this book came from Celine Costello Daly after she participated in a long personal retreat at Gaia House, a retreat centre in south Devon, England. Celine spent much time selecting and polishing transcribed sections from talks, and sending them by e-mail from her home in India. It was extraordinarily kind of her to help me with this book since she now has two very young children to raise.

I wish to thank Gill Farrer-Halls for so carefully reading the typescript through and Anne Ashton, my secretary, for her ongoing work. Their support has been invaluable. I also wish to express appreciation to Judith Kendra of Rider Books for encouraging me to submit a second book. Much appreciation goes to Nshorna, my wonderful daughter, Gwanwyn Williams, her mother, and my mother and late father. I also wish to thank fellow Dharma teachers at Gaia House, especially Christina Feldman, Sharda Rogell and Stephen and Martine Batchelor for their many years of Dharma service.

In the book, I have included a number of stories that I have told over the years. I have purposely changed some minor details in order to preserve their subject's anonymity. I have expanded on some of the themes in this book in *Light on Enlightenment, The Green Buddha* and *The Profound and the Profane*.

ACKNOWLEDGEMENTS

Finally, my heartfelt thanks goes out to the numerous people around the world who give me support with regard to serving the Dharma. I regard the Dharma as the finest teaching available on Earth.

*May all beings live in peace*
*May all beings live in harmony*
*May all beings be fully enlightened*

# An Awakened Life

# INTRODUCTION

At the age of twenty-two I joined the hippy trail to India. On my journey I read one or two books on Buddhism, along with various others much loved by hippies at that time, including *Dharma Bums* and *On the Road* by Jack Kerouac, the Zen writings of Alan Watts, and the work of Aldous Huxley, especially *Island*. I had been in India for some days when I went to Benares, India's most sacred city (now called Varanasi), and then to nearby Sarnath, where the Buddha gave his first talk following his full awakening.

I went into a small Buddhist temple. At the entrance there was a table on which were a number of small, inexpensive books on Buddhism. I chose two and quickly thumbed my way through the pages. I decided to purchase them and sat down in the afternoon sun in the lovely gardens of Sarnath and began reading. Two points that the Buddha addressed in his teachings (known as Dharma) struck me clearly. One was the importance of understanding the nature of impermanence. The Buddha said that whatever arises will pass, whatever comes will go. We live in this world between birth and death. The second point follows on from the first: nothing is worth clinging to because everything is impermanent. To hold on to and identify with the transitory generates suffering and problems at the expense of wisdom.

I had been hitchhiking and taking buses through many countries for more than six months: I was experiencing change from day to day, outwardly and inwardly. In order to move on to the next place I had to let go of the last one. These experiences of daily transition obviously contributed to my receptivity to the Buddha's teachings.

For the next two years I deepened my awareness and understanding of moment-to-moment changes. Such awareness reminded

1

me not to cling to anything, or it would generate anguish in the mind. Then I entered a Buddhist monastery in Thailand and became a monk for the next six years.

Looking back it might be appropriate to describe these experiences as moments of awakening. We can turn our attention to the past and recall various highs and lows that we have experienced and see them as turning points in our lives that have influenced our values and direction. Sometimes, however, it is difficult to realise the significance of a particular moment at the time it is happening.

Our mind has the capacity to develop receptivity to these moments of awakening, and we might be more receptive than we think. It is my intention in this book to offer a wide range of reflections, stories and insights to contribute to your awakening.

It can be useful to see awakening as occurring in two different ways: at the relative level and at the ultimate level. Both are used frequently in the Buddhist tradition. The account of my experience at Sarnath is awakening at the relative level, when insights turned consciousness in a particular direction. It established me further along the path of understanding. Of course, I was deeply interested in that path already, and the Sarnath experience became one of the signposts along the way that contributed to enlightening my life. Such insights make a tangible difference to our existence. We are able to flow on with our daily life while remaining faithful to the original points of awakening.

One of the difficult features of awakening at the relative level is the way that our later thoughts can suffocate the original insight. There are the moments that act as a turning point. We then begin to think and think about the insight. We get bogged down in the thoughts, unable to distinguish the original insight from our thoughts and projections about it. The streams of thought seem to take away the authority of the insight. If we develop a natural appreciation of awakening, this enables an energy to manifest which is expressed as a commitment to the core message of what was revealed to us. This gives us the passion to follow through with our insights.

Ultimate awakening is of a different order altogether. The Buddha's night of enlightenment under the Bodhi tree in Bodh Gaya, Bihar, India, has probably become the best-known account of ultimate awakening in human history. There is often a misunderstanding about what happened on that night, despite the Buddha's comprehensive description of his experience. It was then that the Buddha realised the core issues of human experience. He saw what drove people on from one thing to another and the consequences of such behaviour. He formulated this into a simple but profound teaching based on what he referred to as the Four Noble Truths. These are:

1   There is suffering in the world.
2.  Suffering arises due to conditions. Desire is a primary condition.
3.  There is liberation from the rounds of suffering.
4.  There is a way to end suffering through a noble way of life, namely the Eightfold Path.

Some people believe the Buddha escaped into an absolute realm and that this was his experience of awakening or enlightenment, but this is not the case. He became the Buddha – the Awakened One – due to his comprehensive insights into the human condition. The Buddha refused to become an absolutist proclaiming an absolute state. Nowhere in the twenty volumes of his teachings do we find that kind of approach. In ultimate awakening there is liberation, fulfilment, a deep sense of joy and an understanding of the conditionality of things. The mind is purged of its desire to pursue more and more to try to gain satisfaction for the self.

It is, of course, all too easy to misunderstand what this means. This ultimate awakening does not mean a rejection of the world or a withdrawal from it. In an awakened life, our heart is open, steady and purposeful. We contribute to wise and clear action in the events of our daily life. We are most effective when our inner life isn't bound up in the world of I, me and my with its accompanying egotism.

I remember years ago leading a retreat in the Thai Monastery in Bodh Gaya, India, the village where the Buddha was enlightened. More than 130 people from around the world take part in these retreats. The schedule is intensive, beginning before dawn and lasting until late at night. For some people, such a retreat acts as a turning point in their life. On this particular one, there was a young man from Germany who had a number of profound experiences during the twenty days. He left the retreat feeling that he was fully awakened, liberated, and that his ego had dissolved as a result of his experiences and insights. To his credit, he did not boast about his experiences or make claims to other people. He knew that a major shift had taken place in his life and that the suffering bound up with the ego had dropped away.

Several months went by. He continued to feel at peace with himself. His friends also noticed the changes within him – he was more tolerant, kinder, and wiser about daily life. As time went by, he gradually began to notice that his ego began to grow again, especially after his return to the West. He began experiencing fears about financial security, worrying about his life in Germany and finding fault with others.

Two or three years later, he came to see me when I was teaching in Germany. He told me: 'I left your retreat in India honestly believing I was fully awakened. After a couple of years back in Europe, I realised that I hadn't changed as much as I thought I had. I realise I can't stay awake in the present by relying on my past experiences.'

There are many ways to help yourself to stay awake in the midst of daily life. These include contact with conscious people, mindful living, meditation, inquiry, taking risks and contemplative reading. These themes and others are addressed throughout this book. Receptivity to contemplative reading varies considerably according to our mood, concentration and interest. We have all had the experience of reading the same text more than once, and appreciating the content differently on different occasions.

I believe that this principle particularly applies to reading as a contribution to awakening. We need to read mindfully and slowly. The spiritual journey is both long and short, running essentially from head to heart. It's a long journey when things take time to sink in deeply. It's a short journey when what passes through the head goes straight to the heart and awakens us. In practical terms, this may mean reading *An Awakened Life* mindfully and slowly on a regular basis.

Through such reading, the passages in this book can be a resource in daily life. For that to happen requires both receptivity in the reader and wisdom in the text. I hope that I have fulfilled this latter task. I have no wish to convert readers to Buddhism, only to contribute to living with wisdom.

It was more than thirty years after my first visit that I received an invitation from the Lord Abbot of the Thai Monastery in Sarnath to give teachings in his monastery. It is rather mysterious in the scheme of life how the cycle of events comes around in a full circle.

Christopher Titmuss
Totnes, Devon, UK

*May all beings live with wisdom.*
*May all beings be awakened.*
*May all beings live an enlightened life.*

# THE OPENING OF THE HEART

# THE EMPTINESS OF BUSYNESS

*Stress is a publicly acceptable word for living imprisoned by desire and fear. Stress is the desire to get things done, and the fear of not getting them done.*

In our over-productive society, we have become rather proud of how many labour- and time-saving gadgets we have. Our homes have become filled with them. Technology makes us more efficient and sophisticated in the way we move from one place to another, and the way we communicate. Yet we have no time for any real communication, person to person, face to face.

We don't want people knocking on our front door without a prior appointment. So they telephone and get a disembodied voice, which says 'Thank you for your call. Please leave a brief message after the signal'. We relate to our world and each other in all manner of time-saving ways. But the rather harsh reality is that we have even less time on our hands and we are busier than ever before. Despite our time-saving gadgets, we never have a moment to spare for each other. Friends and loved ones often overstay their welcome.

The busyness of going from one thing to another without a break is an incredibly strong pattern. It fills our existence, so we have produced a convenient and comfortable word to describe it. We call it stress. We have created a huge consumer industry to deal with stress. We go to the gymnasium to work off our stress. We produce a whole range of clothing for various stress-reducing activities. We buy books on stress. We pay expensive psychotherapists to help us deal with stress in our day-to-day life. We go overseas for a holiday. We go to terribly expensive workshops. We go on retreats.

Temporary relief from stress is not a release from stress. We live in a world full of self-deception, believing we will be better off if we increase our workload. We become more productive, yet we don't become happier or wiser as a result. The extraordinary thing about our busyness is that we like to boast about it: 'I'm terribly busy at the moment. I've got so much to do.' There's a certain pride in it: 'I've got such a busy life. The phone never stops ringing.' We have countless letters to write, appointments to keep, places to go. It gives us the feeling that we're important.

We have become so used to this way of life that we hardly have time or energy for anything else. We come home in the evening and turn the television on. We remain glued to the box throughout the entire course of the evening. We barely have enough energy to turn the television off, but have the arrogance to call this 'living in the real world'. If we really realised our plight, then we would find ways to transform our circumstances.

We lie down at night, but our mind is like an old car engine. After a long drive in an old car on a hot day, the motor will often keep going even after pulling out the ignition key. Sometimes our mind is like that at the end of the day, though we certainly want to turn it off so we can sleep. The customary glass of wine is not doing the job for us, so when we lie down, the engine of the mind still turns over and over. We might ask ourselves in the middle of the night, 'Is this what my life is – stress, busyness, hurrying, going from one thing to another?' Stress has become our way of being, our normal lifestyle, and we don't want to admit that we are neurotic and out of touch with the real world. It is a publicly acceptable word for living imprisoned by desire and fear. Stress is the desire to get things done, and the fear of not getting them done. It runs through our psyche. We say, 'I've got so much to do. If I don't get it done, perhaps I'll lose the job or the contract. They want me to finish this job by a certain date. I only have so much time and I'm not sure if I'll get the job finished. I never have enough time.'

Part of the motivation driving us into this fragmented way of living includes feeling we will achieve something. It is the result that matters. Is it? The result – the effect of what we do – becomes another cause for activity. We have no time to experience the fruits of our efforts. No sooner has one task finished than we are on to the next. Success is the spark for the next objective. We say to ourselves, 'As soon as I finish this job, I'm going to have some breathing space. I'm going to take it easy. There's going to be some sanity in my life.' Not much hope of that.

Stress has a momentum to it, and making promises to ourselves about the future springs from stress, not wisdom. We are running around in circles, not getting anywhere. And running around in circles won't make our mind wise either. No sooner do we complete one activity than we start up another. We take a few days holiday and come back full of good intentions, but the momentum starts all over again. There is internal and external pressure to succeed.

What has to happen to make you change? There is a little bit of you that says you must change but the rest of you takes no notice. Are you willing to explore your potential for a stress-free and genuinely contented existence while going about your daily tasks? Or are you going to wait until you have a nervous breakdown, a health crisis, a marriage on the rocks, or simply feelings of despair? Are you determined to carry on as before despite the endless feedback that you are driven, workaholic or obsessed? Or are you going to start today with one basic change? If so, what is it going to be?

# STARTING ALL
# OVER AGAIN

*For consciousness to evolve, we must commit ourselves to living
a conscious life. To know ourselves, to go deep into ourselves,
awakens the mind.*

Knowledge and theories about wisdom are like carrying books on
the back of a donkey. We may carry around many ideas of worthwhile changes that we would like to make in our life. To evolve, we
must put those ideas into practice or they will become a weight for
us. We need to look into every area of our daily existence. It would
be a pity to live an unexamined life and only rely upon external
voices of authority and our inner conditioning to tell us what matters and what to do with our life. For consciousness to evolve, we
must commit ourselves to living a conscious life. To know ourselves, to go deep into ourselves, awakens the mind.

The world presents itself here and now as it comes through our
senses to meet our mind. Through this contact with what's around
us, we create a world of likes and dislikes. We accept one thing and
reject something else. So, not surprisingly, we place all sorts of
demands on the world and the world, in turn, places demands upon
us. What if ultimately the true nature of things is utterly different
from the way we *think* it is? Perhaps we carry around problems
because we have got it all wrong. We think things are one way and
they are not. If we sleepwalk through life, we keep bumping into
walls. To awaken is to change all of that.

We may have to begin our life again to develop a true relationship with life, and to do this we would need to start afresh and treat
all our personal history and accumulated knowledge as having a
minor relevance. In this new beginning, everybody would be new

12

to us, even our family and friends. We would sit, walk, stand and recline mindfully, and take an interest in what was happening in daily life. Mindfulness and insight would be essential features to ending habits and old conclusions that burden daily life.

We would respond to what is with fresh attention. We would treat everyone and everything in the same conscious way, so there would be no prejudice in favour of myself, who is opposed to others. In the circus of life, we learn to ride two horses named Self and Other. If we can't, we have problems. We would not place ourselves before or after others, nor consider ourselves higher or lower than them. There would be nothing to prove.

Not relying on memory, we would experience an inner freedom to look afresh at each day. We would not claim that one moment was more important than another. There would be a genuine sense that every relationship to anything matters, not just a few that the self has selected. There would be no pressure to make others conform, since we would place no demands on them.

Holding the past lightly, we would respond in a different way to the events around us, being less judgemental and invasive. Not having the past to draw upon to keep justifying ourselves, we would observe and listen. Absence of a conditioned view of ourselves means absence of ego with its accumulated needs. We would have evolved out of the obsessions of the self. Living in right relationship means living moment to moment without being imprisoned in the old way of seeing. We would learn about the behaviour of others without being swept away by what they did or didn't do.

In order to be in the moment, we would have the capacity to travel freely and clearly from one situation to another. With nothing remaining constant for a single moment, we would respect the process of life without imposing our conditioning upon it. We would realise it is impossible to make the world conform to our personal wishes.

Far too many authorities propound their theories of progress and evolution with religious certainty. They forget that a thousand probabilities do not make a truth. Imposing their views upon us, they tend to write and speak with certainty their claims about the place of human beings in the scheme of things. From another perspective, it is surely questionable whether we are evolving as long as we continue to be selfish and act aggressively towards others.

Surely a wise relationship to existence is evidence of our evolution, not the ability to produce sophisticated technology or secure an honours degree at a top university.

We have a remarkable capacity to wake up, to meet life fully without riding on the back of hopes and fears. Nobody can make this journey to awakening for us. We have to take a good hard look at our life for authentic change.

# BARE BONES

*'All that I see is none other than myself, but with a different name and form.'*

There are four important facts of physical experience – birth, ageing, sickness and death – and they all involve pain and limitation (including birth, which is rarely an easy passage). We live knowing that there is a beginning to life and an end to it. We all experience this time and neither birth nor death are ever very far away from us. We exist between these two poles. When we die, we can take nothing with us. Death brings the total range of our experiences and contacts to completion. Life complements death and death complements life, and they are as inseparably related as trees are to wood. Reflecting on this puts all the activities of our body, speech and mind into perspective.

During my years as a Buddhist monk, I had the privilege of spending the best part of a year in a cave on an island off the coast of Thailand. One day a young Thai, in his early twenties, came to see me. He wanted to get to New Zealand. Could I help him? I wrote a letter of introduction for him to the New Zealand Embassy in Bangkok.

A few days later his father came to see me with tears in his eyes. He asked me to come with him to the nearby village. When we arrived, he pointed to his son, the young man I had met a few days before. The young man was dead, lying on a bamboo mat, with five bullet wounds in his chest. His father said he had got into a shouting match in the local police station. The police officer lost control and shot the young man dead. Circumstances can snuff out our life very easily and quickly, simultaneously destroying our dreams for the future.

Every one of us passes through a range of experiences and, in a way, every experience has birth and death in it. Wise reflection takes an overview of the flow of life, acknowledging daily the bare bones of existence. In moving through life, each one of us will experience some form of suffering. To look deeply into this matter of life and death puts much of our brief experience on earth into perspective. It makes us more sensitive to what is happening in our own life and in the lives of others.

We act as though we will live forever. There is a peculiar notion in our minds that our life is immortal. Outwardly we refute this notion, but the way we go on living seems to endorse it. It is as if we know we will die but we live as if we won't. Getting down to the bare bones means that we know we will die and we live knowing it. It brings a different kind of perspective to daily life. Such a view, when properly understood, does not generate a depressed feeling but rather enlivens our participation in daily life.

In Buddhist monasteries there are frequent reminders to monks, nuns and laypeople of the imminence of death. There are corpses of men, women and children kept in glass cases. There are paintings depicting the stages of life – from birth to the age of ten years, ten to twenty, and so on up to the age of 100 years. These paintings are a vivid reminder of the ageing process from babyhood to youth, then on to old age, and the deterioration of the body in the very last years. All of us move through this sequence moment to moment. It is so easy to say, 'It is so obvious. I know this already.' The obvious is not necessarily obvious.

My Dharma teacher, the abbot of a well-known monastery in Thailand, the Venerable Ajahn Buddhadasa, regularly began his public talks with the memorable phrase: 'Dear Brothers and Sisters in Birth, Ageing, Pain and Death.' This reminded us all that we have much more in common than we have separating us. Reflection means taking into account and embracing the totality of our life from birth to death. We can make the journey of life an authentic experience for learning and insight.

There is a statement that I have found very helpful over the years: 'All that I see is none other than myself, but with a different name and form.' When we have that kind of awareness, we see that although other people are apparently different, we have more similarities than differences. When we are in touch with ourselves and our own inner silence, we can feel very close to other people. They no longer seem so radically different from us and we feel a sense of fellow participation in the unfolding process between birth and death that permeates our being. We understand that what affects others, affects us. Where there is wisdom, there we find the mind of the Buddha.

# Unstoppable Friendship

*What love requires is the willingness to know and understand
intimately the conditions for the arising of suffering and a
commitment to resolving a problematic existence.*

There are numerous stories that tell how compassion has been
expressed in this world through the centuries. One involves a
young doctor in India who saw a leper lying by the side of the road
as he was driving to the hospital. He got out of his jeep and had a
conversation with the leper. Then he picked him up, put him in the
jeep and continued on to the hospital. By chance, a Brahmin saw
this encounter and couldn't believe his eyes. He followed the jeep
and watched the doctor carry the leper into the hospital. The
Brahmin went in and said to the doctor, 'In my religion, we can't
touch these people. We believe that is the leper's karma and we
should not interfere with it. I'm amazed that you take the risk of
picking this leper up and bringing him here.'

The doctor replied, 'This isn't me. This is Christ's love.' The
Brahmin was moved by these words and said, 'I know a lot about
Christianity since I studied it in school and went to a Catholic col-
lege. Now I understand what is meant by Christ's love. We have
the same message in our tradition when Krishna says that the self
of one person is the same self for all. Yet you stopped to pick the
leper up and I didn't.'

Why do some people find it easy to live with an open heart and
others cannot? It comes out of awareness and deep sensitivity, and
from looking directly at the actualities of life. True friendship
extends itself in all directions, knowing no boundaries. It is a
powerful force for healing and change. I go to India every year. It

is easy to feel repulsed when facing the sicknesses that afflict the desperately poor there; to turn your attention away and look towards something easier on the eye. I find myself criticising the Brahmin belief about untouchables, yet we apply a similar code of avoidance in the West: we hide suffering, sickness and death away. Nothing is hidden in India. It is an 'in your face' world. We can either wake up to the existence of suffering or live like a tortoise withdrawing at the first sign of difficulty.

Authentic love comes from a mind that doesn't turn away. It comes from a mind that faces the possibility of not getting what we want, of losing what we have and being separated from whom and what we love. It doesn't require any special method, technique or training. Nor does it require adopting a religious or philosophical message. What love requires is the willingness to know and understand intimately the conditions for the arising of suffering and a commitment to resolving a problematic existence.

What we see, hear or read may touch our heart, but this inner response may fade quickly as other priorities and concerns enter our mind. It ought to be obvious that a simple feeling may lack the power to bring about action. Making a difference to situations requires a strong and steadfast intention so that there is substance to the feeling of love and concern. Love then has the flavour of authenticity, and we are capable of responding wisely to painful circumstances. We need to be willing to be available and supportive.

Our diverse religious and secular cultures give us enough reminders about love, from the commandment to love thy neighbour to the romantic love celebrated in songs, novels and films. We assume that to give love means we will receive it from our God or others or both. We then quickly forget the importance of being loving in the first place. Love does not belong to the marketplace; it is not a transactional business. We need to be willing to let it flow from within us out to others without wanting a return. If we lean upon another – relying on them for a reciprocal return of the same quality of love – we are in danger of falling flat on our face.

It is an extraordinary thing to feel the power of love, to make life as much as possible one long act of unstoppable friendship. It is a remarkable thing to offer friendship without regard for any personal benefit. If we are going to live this way, our love needs the support of the wisdom of non-attachment and non-dependency, either on a God or others.

Sometimes we rely on religious beliefs and acts of worship to help us through painful periods concerning other people, but it is something of a high-risk strategy to believe that such approaches will get us through the worst nightmares. If we wish to lead a genuinely awakened life, we may well have to open our minds to teachings and practices outside our respective faiths. Sometimes we are reluctant to do this. We feel we are betraying what we have invested so much faith in. To explore does not mean a loss of faith: it is an act of faith to open our heart. If we are open to this exploration, we can experience a genuinely deep love without limitations. That's what counts. That's what we need to be very clear about.

# FEAR

*When we drop our resistance to fear and allow ourselves to feel it,
without holding on to it, we can experience an inner opening
instead of holding back.*

When I stay at Bodh Gaya in India, I tell stories to the children in
the main temple. One day I told them about a group of children
who went on a long walk into the forest at dusk. In the forest, they
saw a huge monster with big eyes, big arms and long claws at the
end of its fingers. They were so frightened that they ran away. The
monster began to grow according to the degree of their fear. As
they were running away, they turned, looked quickly over their
shoulders and saw that the monster kept growing bigger and bigger. As they got more terrified, the monster grew even bigger. All
the children kept running except for one who stopped and faced
the monster: she had decided not to run away.

This little girl began to walk towards the monster, looking it
straight in the eye. As she walked towards the monster, it began to
get smaller and smaller. Then the other children stopped and
looked at the monster, too. They also saw that the monster began
to shrink in size as they walked towards it. It was not long before
the children could hold the monster in the palm of their hands.

The children loved the story. There is much fear and insecurity in their villages. Fear inflates issues. Fear haunts our existence,
and we experience the monsters created in our mind due to past
and present situations. We do ourselves a disservice when we flee
from a monster, even if we think there is no alternative. Let me
make one thing clear: we *can* abide fearlessly. We do not have to live
in the shadow of fear. We do not have to compromise our life
through living in fear of any feature of existence. We are not limited
to learning how to make fear easier to handle, or living in such a

way that fear only touches us from time to time under certain circumstances. We have the potential for living completely free from
fear. When fear speaks, wisdom veils its face.

Fear stops us from becoming liberated, and from taking clear
and direct action. Sometimes we are hardly aware of the occasions
when fear dominates what we do or don't do. We are so used to it
that we have no sensation of fear in our body or mind. We have lost
contact with the sensation, even though the force of fear moves our
life in particular directions, in both the short and long term.

Fear can shape our thoughts, and influence our speech and
actions. For example, we often do not communicate something
important to another person because we are not sure what his or her
reaction will be – fear has determined our decision not to speak out,
although we might not recognise it. We can spend a large amount
of our lives unable to act because we are afraid of the consequences.

Sometimes our defences drop away – through mindfulness,
inquiry, concentration, and exploration. We start seriously on a
journey of exploration into the nature of fear. We explore the fear
of things not changing, and of them changing, no matter how great
or small. Although it may not seem that way at the time, feeling fear
can actually be healthy since this inner sensation shows us what we
have to work with. As long as our defences are up, we do not know
the material that we have to work with. Sensing fear in our chest
and guts, feeling it permeate our cells and dominate our thoughts,
we are in touch with the raw material and can begin our work.

What is it to be afraid? We solidify fear through our thoughts,
images, and ideas. Can we just explore the feeling of being afraid
and regard it for what it is – a collection of unpleasant sensations –
ruthlessly aware that these are just unpleasant sensations? Can we
observe them manifesting through the cells of our body and permeating our conceptual world? When we drop our resistance to
fear and allow ourselves to feel it *without holding on to it*, we can
experience an inner opening instead of holding back. Then these
unpleasant sensations lose their power to stop appropriate action of
body and mind.

There is great potential for liberating insights in the face of
fear. When we are in an unexpected situation that appears to pose
a threat, fear immediately arises and ripples through our bodies and
thoughts. If we can witness that sensation and be wholly with it as

a clear, distinct, deeply unpleasant and disturbing sensation, we may begin to see pockets of light within it and sense its solidity breaking up. That is very liberating.

Our willingness to walk towards the monster of fear can overcome resistance, denial, or rejection. We open the doors of perception. In Hindu and Buddhist countries there are large, fierce-looking statues flanking the entrances of temples and monasteries. They are symbolic – if we remain afraid, we are denied entrance to the Divine. Do we have the courage to explore these monsters? Can we be in touch with fear and still pass through the gates into the breathtaking inner sanctuary of the mystery of life? Being trapped by fear hides access to what is most precious.

# THREE TERRIBLE
# KARMAS

*Despite the fact that there is a painful price when we find
ourselves sucked into their whirlpool, we feel a compelling
attraction to beauty, fame and wealth.*

Like most people, I like to be reasonably well informed, but I don't
buy a newspaper every day. I don't find it inspiring to read daily
accounts of people's problems from every walk of life. So I subscribe to a weekly news publication called *The Week*. I feel it keeps
me reasonably up to date with the main events of the week, and I
sometimes watch the evening news on BBC television when I am
cooking dinner for my daughter and myself.

I read one piece in this weekly news magazine that made me
smile. A reporter met the young, handsome and very successful
Hollywood actor, Brad Pitt. Brad Pitt asked the reporter: 'Do you
know what the three terrible karmas are in Buddhism?' After a brief
silence, he then replied to his own question: 'Beauty, fame and
wealth. They're the things that stop you finding true happiness.'

After I read the piece, I thought, 'He's right. Very terrible
karma.' The media constantly pursue information about Brad Pitt's
personal life. There is endless gossip. Within his profession, there is
envy and jealousy. His celebrity status travels with him everywhere.

In our more detached moments, we might agree with this
Buddhist viewpoint. However, these moments of recognising this
simple truth tend to be very fleeting, because the desire for these
three karmas in our lives then takes over. Despite the fact that there
is a painful price when we find ourselves sucked into their
whirlpool, we feel a compelling attraction to beauty, fame and
wealth.

There are plenty of investigative journalists looking behind the closed doors of those trapped in these 'three jewels' of secular culture and reporting back to us on their personal lives. It ought to be obvious to us that their lives seem more messy, complicated and confused than the rest of us. Yet we delude ourselves into imagining that they are full of excitement and always upbeat – that superficial needs, loneliness and despair don't really enter their world.

If we determinedly put aside all craving for beauty, fame and wealth, we may find our life moving towards wisdom and compassion. We would spend less time and money on our appearance, and less time trying to impress others. Beauty's sister is vanity. We wouldn't be thinking up ideas how to preserve our looks, increase our reputation or make even more money, because these concerns would be put aside. Others have drowned in their self-indulgence in these three areas, wasting their life trying to be something they are not.

We have to take an honest look at our situation, as the last thing we want is to end up like those people. It is worthwhile to take the concerns of the Buddha seriously, since these 'three karmas' stop us from realising true happiness. The Buddha knew what he was talking about. Before his renunciation, he lived as Prince Siddhartha Gautama in the country of Sakya. He was a handsome young man, aged twenty-nine, married to the most beautiful woman of the land, the raven-haired Yasodhara. People idolised him. Wherever he walked the citizens threw petals at his feet. He had great wealth, including countless servants and three palaces, one for each season – winter, summer and monsoon. It took a personal crisis not long before his thirtieth birthday for him to turn his back on the three terrible karmas of beauty, fame and wealth.

Brad Pitt's chiselled good looks and ability to act – to pretend to be somebody he isn't – have certainly brought him fame and fortune. In return for losing the sweet pleasure of being free to walk the streets anonymously, I hope he gains a great opportunity for discovery. If he continues to keep his view alert about these karmas, he won't feel a tinge of regret about the passing of his natural beauty, his fan worship and substantial salary. If he knows the emptiness of it all, then true happiness can become his.

Brad Pitt is right. Yes, terrible karma.

# SMALL GESTURES

*We cannot always summarily dismiss what bothers us. We may have power over the life of a mosquito, but we don't have power over the minds of others or the ebb and flow of existence.*

While I was at the monastery in Thailand, an American lecturer came to stay. He wanted to increase his understanding of himself and his relationship to the world. He thought of himself as an intellectual and felt cut off from much of the rest of himself. After he had been there for some days, I noticed that he was leaning head first into the toilet adjoining his room. As I came closer, I saw that he had put a leaf in the water. He said, 'When I came to use the toilet, I noticed an ant floating down there. I'm trying to rescue it.'

Whether he was aware of it or not, he was actively expressing his heart's connection with a small sentient being. When we understand our connection with the life around us, it shows itself in such small and apparently insignificant gestures. We hear a lot about very powerful meditations – tantric, yogic, kundalini, chakra and others – but they don't hold a candle to the power of loving kindness. Responding to the plight of other sentient beings shows that the heart is expanding beyond the limitations of the intellect.

When we are caught up in our habitual patterns, we block access to loving kindness, no matter how cool, efficient and productive we may appear to others or ourselves. If we concentrate in daily life on loving kindness, our heart will expand, and such a focus will contribute to our awareness and understanding of the interconnection of all life. Inner joy is a natural outcome of a commitment to respect our connection with daily circumstances rather than living in fantasies.

At night in the monastery the mosquitoes came out. The tendency of the lecturer and most other people would be to kill any found in their hut. One day the lecturer realized that there would always be irritants circulating in his life. Mosquitoes in life take many forms. He decided not to kill them, but to learn to coexist with them as a practice in keeping the heart steady in the face of being pestered. We cannot always summarily dismiss what bothers us. We may have power over the life of a mosquito, but we don't have power over the minds of others or the ebb and flow of existence.

It would be easy to conclude that such practices entail some romantic and idealistic notion of preserving all life, no matter what. Such a view would prevent the swamp close to a village that contains malaria-infected mosquitoes being cleaned out, so we have to make difficult decisions in terms of what should be allowed to live and what shouldn't. It is hard to find much merit in the existence of a mosquito, but if we look at our relationship to a mosquito metaphorically, we can learn about ourselves.

Our actions affect insentient life as well as sentient: we can practise expressing heartfelt gratitude to the things we use, for example. As we become more aware, we notice when we are insensitive towards any aspect of creation, and how that denies us the opportunity to fully participate in existence. When we become more aware of what we see, hear and do, we are happy to engage in actions that seem inconspicuous in the scheme of things. The inner expression of the heart shows itself in these small outward gestures.

We must keep faith with this approach. In our day-to-day practice, we might simply remind ourselves of the ancient Buddhist injunction, 'May all beings live in peace and harmony'. Saying this is not just a convenient way to end a meditation, but an expression of an inner intention to open out consciousness to embrace all forms of life. In addition, this practice is about opening our consciousness to the way life is, not how we would like it to be.

Mindfulness contributes to our capacity to make small gestures. For more than 2,500 years the Buddhist tradition has highlighted the importance of mindfulness. Some of the schools have concentrated on mindfulness as a primary vehicle for wisdom. There are books and books of practices based on mindfulness. The Buddha provided teachings and endorsement for this way of practice. One of the ways employed currently to remind us to stay mindful concerns bell-ringing. It may be the front-door bell, a church bell, the telephone or a bell announcing a time for meditation. Upon hearing the bell, we stop for three or four seconds for the practice of just listening.

Such a mindfulness exercise sounds very simple and is certainly easy to implement. It is one thing to practise this on a daily basis and it is something else to suddenly stop the mind in its tracks. We are often caught up in a headlong flow of activity, going from one thing to another. To suddenly stop, totally arrest the movement of our mind and body, brings us back to the present moment. We can then pick up the telephone mindfully and respectfully.

# NEGATIVITY

*Our ego gets into an ugly habit of deliberately putting other people down. In fact, we may even find ourselves behaving similarly to the people we rush to condemn.*

There was a small group meeting to discuss the plight of a besieged ethnic minority in one part of Europe. They were considering appropriate steps to try to give support to this group of people. During the meeting, one person offered some views and opinions that made some others in the group squirm. She said that she worked as an aid worker and had met, on a number of occasions, people from this ethnic minority. She said that they had a reputation for causing trouble and had very little respect for the nation who had taken them in as refugees.

The woman spoke matter-of-factly. She didn't sound negative, hostile or racist. She probably thought she was being quite objective. Probably most of us express such remarks about certain groups of people. The fact is that our generalised statements perpetuate problems. There was nobody from this ethnic minority at the meeting who could respond to the woman's remarks. Nobody at the meeting made any comment. One or two people glanced across at each other, expressing momentary concern through their eyes. It takes vigilance to observe the ways we use labels and fix impressions.

If we look into our own minds, we can see that the unhealthy aspects of ourselves often show up in our contact with others. When we find problems with another person, we only see the gross extensions of their personality. It's easy to forget that we are concentrating on just one or two aspects of them. We then use these impressions to support a fixed and hostile view. In time, our heart becomes cold or heated with anger, and our ego gets into an ugly habit of deliberately putting other people down. In fact, we may even find ourselves behaving similarly to the people we rush to condemn. Through the practice of calm attention, we can learn to witness gross movements of our mind, so we won't entangle these states of mind with what we see or hear. As we observe another person with awareness and interest, we can distinguish the gross from the subtle expressions of their personality. We begin to notice what we have in common. We can also keep in touch with the changing features of the person. The inner person shares the same characteristic as us, namely heart, mind and body.

To see what we have in common takes priority, and when we understand that, an underlying warmth manifests in our relationship to others. Then the unhealthy features of another's personality have no power to trigger a similar state of mind in ourselves. Though certain actions of others remain disagreeable to us, we intuitively understand where their negativity is coming from. When we become caught up in others' behaviour, it hinders access to wise action. It is letting go of, or overcoming, negativity that paves the way for the resolution of problems.

Out of this quality of true observation comes respect. The word *respect* is derived from the Latin *respicere*, which means to observe. Even a small incident can tell us a lot about ourselves. For example, a person in the meditation hall fidgets, affecting the peacefulness of our mind. We don't realise that it is our mind that is agitating around the bare sound. Respect fades away. We see that we have forgotten to observe. We become negative and resentful. Our reaction reminds us that our inner peace lacks depth in those moments. So we continue our practice of moment-to-moment mindfulness to re-establish a calm, inner connection with what is.

Observation and reflection act as primary conditions for wise responses even in the most difficult of situations. Through the power of clarity, we can overcome whatever life presents. A typical response to this statement is, 'Yes, but how?' We want step-by-step tools, and we want them to work quickly, or we give up. Work on ourselves might be a lifelong undertaking. There ought to be enough messages from within telling us when we are caught up in negativity. It will probably mean practising to overcome minor reactions, and deliberately letting go of events that we normally react against.

Our mind is with us until we die. When we have no peace of mind, we suffer. That ought to be reason enough to practise letting go of negativity, and such a practice will awaken us.

# The Capacity to Love

*How can we blame those who have suffered and then acted out of their own affliction? Aren't we doing the same? Who in the world is there to blame?*

We often find ourselves on the horns of a dilemma. We say noble things about how much we love people, and at the time we mean every word. This feeling for life, and especially compassion for those at the raw end of things matters a great deal: the capacity to love keeps people together. So we express love in generalised ways, but often we cannot show the same love to those who are very close to us. There is a gap, and it is important to bridge that gap. One of the common accusations against people engaged in projects of human service is that such people neglect their loved ones. They are so busy saving the world that they cannot save enough time to be with their family or close friends. If they don't take the responsibility of bridging the gap, such people will rightly be accused of having double standards, of living a hypocritical life.

We are often concerned about people who lack empathy towards other people or animals. They may not blink at going to war, endorsing the slaughter of people, or shooting animals for pleasure while out on hunting trips. Others work in laboratories, dragging animals out of cages to experiment on them in the name of progress. Such people and others seem to lack an emotional connection with suffering in these areas of their lives. They may be warm and considerate to those they identify with, but those outside their narrow circle they treat with utter indifference. The true capacity to love lacks walls. It reaches out to all. It is a sign of authentic emotional health.

We hear a great deal in the Buddha's teachings about the importance of love – but sometimes we simply don't feel loved or loving. When we speculate why we feel like this, we often blame the past – our childhood, our parents, and what others have done to us. When we blame others, we generate and project negativity. The degree to which we solidify this view and point an accusing finger reveals the degree to which we harden ourselves to others. If there is no love, there is no happiness. If there is no happiness, there is no love.

Our relationship to painful situations in the past matters more than the situation itself. In the discovery and rediscovery of ourselves, we become aware not only of what is past, but how we are relating to it. We might hear two quite distinct and different voices within ourselves. We can hear the hard voice – judgemental and condemning. Or we can hear the wise voice, which might intimate that the abusers were probably once abused themselves. They inflict on others what was inflicted upon them. How can we blame those who have suffered and then acted out of their own affliction? Aren't we doing the same? Who in the world is there to blame?

We see that blaming and thoughts of revenge arise from failing to understand patterns and tendencies of mind that dominate people's lives. When we are ill, we can easily sink into worry. Yet sometimes sickness, including life-threatening illnesses, brings the best out of the human spirit. Being unhealthy does not have to become a trigger for heaping unhappiness upon ourselves.

I conducted a moving interview with an Italian mother who had struggled with cancer for many years. She had transformed her painful and life-threatening situation into an instrument for the affirmation of life. She found the capacity to transform a nightmare of pain and suffering into something transcendental. When I asked her how she approached her cancer, she replied that the cancer gave her the possibility to see life and other people. 'My inner life is a workshop where pain and fear can turn into love for every single being who is suffering.'

As she came fully into the present and worked with the pain, she transformed her way of looking at the past. As she began to see more life in the present, she could also see more life in the past. She said, 'I found again all the beautiful things in the past that I hadn't been able to appreciate. I saw very clearly the little child that I was.

I've grown into love and appreciation. Now there is joy.'

It might be appropriate for some people to explore the patterns and conditioning of their past. Others might prefer to show a wholehearted commitment to the present, or deliberately engage with both. The fruit of wisdom is the capacity to live a loving life that surmounts major obstacles. We can express something divine. If for just one moment in our lives we reveal a deep love, our existence will have been worthwhile.

# THE SEXUAL
# REVOLUTION

*There are four simple questions that we might need
to ask ourselves before initiating sexual contact with
another consenting adult.*

A married woman came to participate in one of my US retreats.
Years ago, she had become involved in the so-called sexual revolution, and decided to spend time with a guru in India who advocated free love. Friends warned her that love wasn't free: there was
a cost. Life in the ashram could become emotionally painful and it
was expensive compared to others in India. However, the woman
travelled to India with her husband, who shared the same views
about sexual freedom. They agreed: 'Society has changed. We have
all moved forward. There's no reason why we shouldn't have the
opportunity to pursue other sexual relationships.'

In the ashram they did so-called Tantric workshops, which
involved partner-swapping sexual activities in the name of spiritual
practice. The couple thought they were participating in a new
type of society, but the result was nothing short of disaster.
Intellectually they felt they were sexually liberated, but emotionally a vast storehouse of conflicting feelings was building up.

Upon their return to the West, the woman took an extra partner with the knowledge of her husband, and her husband also took
a lover. This went on for some months. The wife felt pain every
time she thought of her husband touching another woman. The
husband was also resentful of his wife being in the arms of another
man. Yet both had enthusiastically agreed with the concept of
sexual freedom in marriage. The marriage broke up, and they
divorced each other on the grounds of incompatibility. During the

35

retreat, five years later, she told me she was still crying at night. The head can affirm one thing while the heart affirms something else entirely.

Fashionable trends can be destructive. To live sensitively in relationship with others, to recognise how vulnerable we all are, enables us to treat sexuality with great care. A sexual relationship is a powerful human experience. For one partner or the other, or both, sexual communication may be the affirmation of something deep. Feelings are at work in the deepest recesses of our emotions and these beautiful feelings can become aroused during the time of sexual closeness. All too easily, permissive behaviour can reduce people to unfeeling objects, there simply to satisfy physical desire. Eventually, such desires sow the seeds for suffering, either about intimate relationships or in another area of life, such as ageing, feeling unwanted or jealousy.

The issue is not monogamy, polygamy, heterosexuality, homosexuality or bisexuality. What activities cause suffering and what commitments safeguard people from suffering? That concern takes priority. There is a middle ground between cultural and religious rigidity around sexual behaviour between consenting adults, and insensitive and permissive sexual activity that lacks respect for all concerned. For there are qualities of heart that emerge from a healthy attitude to making love, including respect, sensitivity and depth of connection. If we know ourselves, we ought to know where we are coming from in any kind of sexual activity. There are four simple questions that we might need to ask ourselves before initiating sexual contact with another consenting adult. These questions are:

1. Is this the right person?
2. Is this a right choice?
3. Is this the right place?
4. Is this the right time?

If we find that our response is a 'no' to any of these questions, we should listen to that internal alarm. It would be a rare person who never made errors of judgement in expressing their sexual feelings. The pleasure of the activity may be short and the pain of the consequences much longer. We ought to bear in mind before we embark on making love to another. When we make mistakes, it is vital that we learn from them. Sexual feelings are powerful; they easily override common sense. One or two mistakes in this area are a clear signal that we are vulnerable to letting feelings overrule our wisdom.

Sometimes we need to listen to our mind, not our heart. It is vital that we find ways to transform inner pressures before we succumb to basic urges that create chaos in life. If we feel we have got away with something we may feel relieved. That thought then becomes the spark for the same impulsive behaviour. The 'never again' commitment is often short-lived. If we don't want to be burnt, we had better not get too close to the fire.

Everyone would probably agree that sexual energy can act as a powerful force in people's lives. It requires from all of us a great deal of understanding so that we treat each other and ourselves in caring and respectful ways. Through awareness, relaxation and insight, we can know the integration of sexuality with our whole being rather than it being an uncomfortable, separate issue. In that clarity, concerns about being in an intimate relationship or not seem secondary to the value of an awakened life.

# FEELINGS AND
# THOUGHTS

*Every time you think about the past and your cherished job, your
thoughts increase and intensify your pain. Thoughts refuel
painful feelings.*

A feeling itself is often our primary experience and thought,
though it may not seem like it, the secondary one. Out of your feelings about something come your thoughts, and your thoughts
define your feelings and reinforce them. They in turn are rein-
forced by your feelings, and the whole interaction gains a kind of
reality. Let me take an example. You have lost your job. You
experience the shock of that loss, and that pain lasts for a certain
amount of time. Every time you think about the past and your cherished job, your thoughts increase and intensify your pain.
Thoughts refuel painful feelings.

Take another example. A gold ring has been in the family for
three or four generations. The mother passes the ring on to her
daughter. When the daughter becomes a mother, she passes it on to
her child. The ring comes to have much sentimental value. As the
years and decades go by, the family develops an attachment to the
ring. It invests the ring with all kinds of significance that do not
apply to any other gold ring. The accumulation of feelings and
thoughts around the ring carry with them the fear of loss. The
great, great, great-grandmother passed on her gold ring to her
daughter as an act of kindness, and now it has become an object of
attachment.

The ring continues to provide pleasure, but the fear of loss
weighs heavily on the family as well. The daughter says: 'I would
hate to lose it. Sometimes I wake up in the night after having a

nightmare that I lost the ring and couldn't find it anywhere.' The ring itself is a piece of metal. On to this piece of metal are stuck all the family's projections. Is there anything that you are carrying that you would hate to lose?

Another example. A man was interested in being ordained as a Buddhist monk, but decided not to. He had long, flowing hair that had taken years to grow, and didn't want to lose it – by shaving his head – a prerequisite for ordination. He identified with his hair, so he feared to lose it. His feelings and thoughts about his hair mattered more than renunciation. We do not permit ourselves to see an object as an object, an item as an item. We see the object, the item, the relationship to 'me'. So the seeds of unrest begin, instead of seeing whatever we turn our attention to for what it is. Because we project our emotions on to objects, we fuel feelings and thoughts to produce a problem.

We sometimes do not wish to admit to the problem. We want to put it into the back of our mind so that we don't have to deal with it. One of the strategies that we use is to throw ourselves into another activity to avoid dealing with unresolved problems. But there is no escape. We cannot run into one corner of our mind as a way of denying another corner. Our mind is like a web, with perceptions, feelings and thoughts holding everything together. It is vital that we are clear about this even if we cannot see an obvious connection between one activity of our mind and another.

Trying to control our feelings through willpower creates pressure in another area of our life. Yet at times it is necessary to resist external demands that affect us. Resistance is sometimes regarded as a dirty word, but we have the right to resist external oppression such as manipulative, dominating forces. Those forces may be a government, a multinational business, a boss or a family member. Our initial response may be fear. 'I don't want to be disapproved of. It is easier to conform, easier to go along with.' When we suppress our right to speak up, we suppress our voice of freedom. Instead, we conform. We will never feel good about ourselves if we keep holding back from expressing our concerns. Such conformity creates ongoing mistrust in relationships.

Or we can respond with resistance. Wise resistance to oppression means finding skilful means to resolve exploitation and harm. To resist is to stop the destruction of liberty, and this is often necessary in the face of individuals and institutions that cause suffering. Too many individuals fear to resist the demands, beliefs and intolerance of authority figures. They are often pressurised into conforming and when they resist, they are told: 'You're being selfish' or, 'It's just your ego'.

When a friend resisted sexual advances made to her by a Tibetan lama, he told her: 'You're resisting. It's your ego, you are a suppressed personality.' She told me: 'I refused to undress in front of him. I refused to let him give me a massage. He was nothing more than a dirty old man. And I stormed out of his room.' She found out later that other women were not so forthright. They submitted to his advances because they believed him when he claimed they were in denial of their feelings.

When is resistance an act of wisdom and when is it foolish? What do we resist? Do we resist looking at ourselves? Do we resist looking at our mind games? When we become involved in one narrow field of interest, we may be suppressing other equally important areas. This may be apparent to loved ones, but not to ourselves. It is likely to keep us estranged from them and then suppression becomes a part of our life. When something keeps coming up when we're focused on something else we just push it back to keep focused. If something keeps coming up again and again, repeating itself through thoughts, emotions, feelings and desires then our mind is saying: 'Look, don't suppress this. Look at it.'

When we refuse to stop and look then we are on the road to confusion and agitation. Like resistance, suppression is considered in terms of its content. The woman wisely resisted the lama's advances. The lama needs to examine his suppressed sexual urges and their consequences.

# THE PRICE OF
# BEAUTY

*When a woman is told on numerous occasions that she is
beautiful, the words lose all their original meaning. Endless
flattery eventually leads to self-doubt.*

To an alarming degree, we have become infatuated with the super-ficiality of the outward appearance. The hairstyles and clothes, and the size and shape of a person can significantly influence the way we relate to people. We can get caught up in our inner forces of attraction and aversion due to the way we experience the outer appearance of somebody else. Certainly, outer appearance tells us something about their personality, but there is much more to a person than what appears on the surface. Caught up in our like or dislike of their outward appearance, we cannot relate to the whole person but only to their superficial features.

When we focus on our perceptions of beautiful and ugly, we can feel the impact this has on the quality and tone of our communication. Countless magazines showing beautiful men and women, often youthful in appearance, warp our potential to see more deeply. One pop song that reached the top of the charts advised people not to buy such magazines as they 'will only make you feel ugly'.

We tend to treat people differently under the influence of such perceptions, even though the person never asked to be born the way they are. It ought to be obvious to us that physical appearance arises due to parents and genetic background. We forget this and relate to people through their physical attributes rather than their inner being.

Beauty can become a trigger for desire and envy: beautiful men and women can find themselves under various kinds of scrutiny, which makes life unpleasant for them. They may have to hear countless remarks with sexual overtones. When a woman is told on numerous occasions that she is beautiful, the words lose all their original meaning. Endless flattery eventually leads to self-doubt. To be told frequently that you are beautiful often results in feeling not beautiful.

Some men have a constant need to prove themselves. Like little boys, they feel a need to show off, to impress others with their remarks. Women then find themselves on the receiving end of their persuasion, manipulation, or ego trips. The intensification of the male ego into these arrogant mind states can lead to aggression. If one man has a fixation on a beautiful woman there are sure to be others who feel the same.

Beautiful women have told me they experience immediate concerns when a man wishes to enter a conversation with them. 'The first thing that comes up in my mind is: "What is his motive? Is it going to be another hassle?"' Handsome, rich or successful men can experience similar fears.

We men carry around in our heads images from magazines and the cinema of beautiful women. We imagine what it would be like to be very close to such a woman. We wonder why we never see such women out on the street, except on extremely rare occasions. We forget that such beauty mostly exists only on paper and celluloid. Skilled hairstylists, make-up artists, beautiful clothing and camera operators with the appropriate lighting and camera angles enhance the appearance of models and actors.

We find ourselves behaving foolishly in the face of beauty. If you walk down the street with a beautiful woman, you notice how many men and women look her up and down. Different people will look at her whole body or parts of it. Some women will look at her clothes and take a secondary glance at her companion. It can become disconcerting when it happens every few yards.

Unless we are willing to focus on our feelings, to watch them change and understand how we express them, our emotional life will become charged with desire and fantasy. People can find themselves involved in a relationship due to the force of mutual attraction. After a period, this force begins to diminish, and may even be replaced with aversion. One partner or both begin to actively dislike the physical appearance of the other. They focus on this one feature at the expense of the whole person. The pull towards becomes a recoil and there follows a painful struggle to extricate from the relationship.

Some people do this repeatedly. They never learn, leaving a trail of hurt and disappointment behind them. If our emotional life is not steady enough to be able to accommodate the intensity of interpersonal relationships, then we have to accept that fact. If there is too much pain in successive relationships, then perhaps the message is to live independently, to stay clear for a period from intimate involvement with another.

We need to practise watching our feelings arise, stay and pass. We need to be aware of the feelings of others. Through inner clarity, we can attend to the whole person rather than become enamoured with beauty at the expense of a deeper communication. In this way, we pay respect to others, safeguarding ourselves from slipping into unhealthy patterns of attraction and aversion. Such sensitivity leads to a liberated and wise attitude, free from the rigidity of Victorian thinking and the crudeness of permissiveness.

We pay respect to others through an honest appreciation of their qualities and attributes rather than pointless flattery. The difference between the two ought to matter to the recipient.

# SUFFERING

*We do not have to be left unsettled and in anguish, even
when someone we love dies: instead, through meditation,
we can commit ourselves to staying steady on a daily
basis, day by day, hour by hour.*

Stating it simply, life manifests as a field of experience. Suffering is
the primary issue of experience and predominates over all else. An
intelligent way of life considers the nature of suffering in order to
understand its causes and our relationship to it. Buddhist teachings
and practices work to eradicate the weight of suffering inflicted on
human existence. There is the physical suffering of the body
through disease and ageing, and there is the suffering of mind.
When we look at the mind, we see that various factors have contributed to its problems. The word 'suffering' not only applies to
mental problems, but also to minor unrest, upsets and agitations.

I'm sure you have experienced the suffering of a major personal
loss or bereavement. However, at a subsequent date, there may well
come about an intuitive sense that this time of sorrow was one of
the most important periods in your life: 'I learnt something about
myself. I learnt something about life.' Sometimes it is only through
pain that we learn. We're marvellous at becoming philosophers six
months later! When someone else is experiencing a problem, we
can become skilled at giving a whole discourse on how to be and
what to do.

If we meditate and reflect in our daily life, we can respond
wisely to the unexpected loss of somebody dear to us. Formal meditation practice basically consists of sitting still with your back
straight and quietly staying present from one moment to the next.
If it helps, you can focus on your breathing. Meditating like this
regularly contributes significantly to calmness of mind, a steady

presence, and feeling grounded from one moment to the next. We do not have to be left unsettled and in anguish, even when someone we love dies: instead, through meditation, we can commit ourselves to staying steady on a daily basis, day by day, hour by hour. This attitude needs to be present at the time painful events happen if we are to avoid months of suffering before we become wise about a tragedy.

There is also suffering that springs from the force of unthinking emotional reactions to events. You can develop practices that help with moody patterns, such as applying an antidote to the state of mind. For example, you feel angry and you are uncertain what to do with this anger. You meditate on the idea that life is not meant to conform to your wishes. You reflect upon the situation of all human beings undergoing birth, ageing, pain and death. The old have death before their eyes while the young live with it behind their back. Yet time passes equally for all. You reflect on the reasons for the heart to feel loving kindness for another and their circumstances. You reflect on the value of equanimity when things are not going your way.

Therapies and religions may or may not provide methods to transcend unsatisfactory mind-states. Always trying to show loving kindness when we are angry, for example, is of limited use: it can become a form of avoidance. For example, a religious person may turn their attention to their God as a means to transcend their troubling emotions. But God may not be the solution, only a temporary escape. When problems keep coming back, they have to be dealt with directly.

Another common escape from hurt and pain can arise when a long-standing personal relationship ends. You are left with a stack of memories which keep recalling all those days and nights together. It isn't easy to move on from them. An old Chinese proverb reminds us: 'You cannot prevent the bird of sadness from flying over your head but you can prevent it from nesting in your hair.' It's easy to feel trapped in the past and forget how quickly, if you meet somebody new, the memory of the old relationship will lose its power and vanish. The past has been sublimated with somebody new, but rushing into the new relationship may have denied you the opportunity to come to a deeper understanding of the unresolved issues in your old relationship. There is a danger that after a while you will fall back into the old patterns. We watch ourselves to see what arises in relationship to attitude and states of mind. We listen to the voice within indicating avoidance or escape from a previous situation. There is no greater challenge for a human being than to transform personal suffering that is arising here and now.

# THE CHALLENGE
# OF CHANGE

*She felt sick to the stomach, unhappy and confused. She did not
know whether she had made the right decision or not.*

The young woman unexpectedly found herself pregnant. What
made matters worse, she was not completely sure who the father
was. Although she had a regular boyfriend, she had also slept with
another man one night when slightly the worse for drink after going
to a rock concert. The young woman felt too embarrassed to ask the
two men to undergo paternity tests. She could not imagine that
either of them would want to share responsibility for bringing up
the child. Furthermore, she did not feel in any way ready at this
time to take on the task of parenting. She was left with only one
alternative: abortion. At the time, she felt that nothing worse could
have happened to her. Every horse thinks its own pack heaviest.

She made an appointment with a local clinic, quietly termi-
nated the two months' pregnancy and returned back to her flat after
a couple of hours. Nobody knew. Neither her friends, nor her
family. She thought that once she had made the decision, it would
quieten her mind. The abortion was final: there could be no going
back.

The young woman quickly found out that life does not work to
prescription. She felt sick to the stomach, unhappy and confused.
She did not know whether she had made the right decision or not.
She felt guilty for not informing both men, and for not seeking the
counsel of others. Her friends and boyfriend could not fathom out
what was the matter with her. The inner conflict ended their relationship. She cried a lot at night, and was often unsure what she
was crying about.

One of the worst times to make important decisions is when we are agitated and secretive. Secrecy places extra pressure on the mind, and the waves of agitation this provokes are difficult to handle. It is important to share with those whose voices we value whatever we are going through rather than trying to hide things. We often mistakenly believe that we can handle everything by ourselves. We can't, and when we try we find ourselves grasping streams of thoughts, and feeling distressed at the way our mind goes off at all sorts of tangents.

Situations become manageable through a balanced perspective. The mind has a remarkable power to adjust to the unexpected and unwanted if we give it the opportunity. A pregnancy is not the end of the world; it can be the beginning. What seems the worst possible thing to happen in youth can transform into love and gratitude later. Instead of experiencing inner turmoil, we can develop a wise relationship to any new situation that enters our life.

An expansive mind sees and understands the movement, expression and manifestation of change, so that we can live with such awareness in daily life. The unexpected can destroy our best-laid plans. We have to be prepared for that – not live in resistance to it. The marvellous thing is that no perception of a situation stays the same.

Instead, far too often, habits affect our capacity to handle situations. These habits prevent us seeing fresh opportunities. Once we are free from the shadow of such habits, we are open to the sweetness of something vast and unknown. As time went by, the young woman stopped dwelling in the past, and her unhappiness and confusion began to change. She changed careers and went into nursing, and eventually became a midwife in a major city hospital. There is an unfathomable element in life that defies all our attempts to comprehend circumstances. We are going along in one direction, then we find ourselves moving along in another. The young woman's termination of her pregnancy contributed to inspiring her to enable other women to give birth. She could not have planned her life this way.

This element of the unknown moves our life around without us ever having direct access to it. In countless ways, it reminds us of how little control we have over our life in terms of the way our life unfolds. Life could not be any other way. Every time the unexpected occurs, it's a direct reminder to us of the daily influence of the unknown.

This unfathomable element knows neither birth nor death, nor ever changes its essential, all-influencing nature. The young woman could not have possibly foreseen the outcome of her circumstances. The thought of the connection between pregnancy and midwifery never arose. The morning knows not what the afternoon brings.

We have all observed similar situations in our own lives. We say to each other, 'Who would have thought?' The unfathomable element keeps moving us into new directions. We influence the great web of existence and it influences us.

# DISILLUSIONMENT

*The first priority for the student was to relax and enjoy himself,
not to throw away his life studying morning, noon and night.*

A young man was studying psychology at university. At the beginning he enjoyed the course and worked hard. His parents had given him a loan, so he felt obliged to do his best for them, but in the early part of his final year he lost all interest in psychology. He didn't want to go to classes, nor do research, nor switch on his computer. There was nothing much else going on in his life, but his interest dropped away like grains of sand through his fingers. Ironically (since he was studying psychology), the student said he could not understand his own mind.

Whatever we are interested in commands our attention. We refer to a person, news item or game as interesting, transferring our interest from our mind to the object. The more interest we have in whatever we are doing, the more we are able to keep our attention on it. Or so we believe. Interest is not eternal, and not even as continuous as we would wish. If we lack interest in a subject, it is difficult to learn. It is also true that a person who is only interested in one thing will probably find their interest fading away at some point, possibly resulting in complete disillusionment. The student in the story was afraid this would happen to him.

In my view, the first priority for the student was to relax and reflect, not to throw away his life studying morning, noon and night. He said his parents would not like to hear what I said. I told him to take walks, read good novels, talk with friends – to do whatever he felt like doing without behaving stupidly. I told him to treat my response as common sense. Sometimes our interest in studying drops away because deep down we have realised the futility of it. We can't sustain an interest in everything we do, let alone one isolated thing. Absorbing countless concepts ranks as a poor substitute for authentic living.

A single interest in the process of life, including our own, consumes all other secondary interests, including concentrated study. We can develop a passionate interest in what goes on within and without. Those of us who do this are hardly ever bored, and if we are, we examine our state of mind. We look at practical steps we can take, such as bringing more variety into our life; meditating on the preciousness of human existence; and bringing focus and attention to our ordinary activities. In the simplest daily activities, the wise develop their interests while they do the most ordinary things – sitting, walking, eating, washing and so on.

For in that interest we discover the simplicity of life, and a beauty in that simplicity. It causes many problems and anxieties to dissipate, and we experience contentment with what is. If you can catch the spirit of this, you will discover much. Then you will express your true nature through every action.

The student listened to my advice. He returned to university determined to 'have a life' as he said, even though he felt uncomfortable about neglecting his studies. He failed to hand in his papers at the correct time, but he got himself involved in doing things he wanted to do. He started swimming again, reading novels, hanging out longer in the coffee shops, doing yoga and spending more time with friends. He experienced a certain power in his mind from doing what he wanted to do, rather than doing things just to please others. For the first time, he had some sense of himself as a full human being. At first, he felt a bit guilty, feeling he was letting his parents down. He kept reminding himself that he must act as an adult, not as an obedient son.

The student eventually realised the psychology course had little to do with real people. It had more to do with ideas about them. He quit the course, and never regretted it. His parents and tutors told him he was throwing away a golden opportunity to become a psychologist. They didn't understand him when he said he felt he was throwing away his life through studying all the time. At times, he had to remember when meeting his parents that a still tongue made for a wise head.

# OBJECTS OF PLEASURE

*Although our feeling of pleasure may have arisen out of contact with an external object, we must ask ourselves whether that object is necessary in order to feel happy.*

A pleasing object touches our mind through our senses, and creates a psychological impression that provokes our interest and attracts us to it. The intensity of the pleasure determines the strength of our interest. Even when everything in our daily life flows along well, we need to remain alert to sudden changes that can take away all our pleasure in the objects that surround us. True contentment comes through wisdom: our possessions can never offer us lasting satisfaction.

When our search for what gives us pleasure becomes a strong pattern in our lives, we find that we are obliged to move repeatedly towards the same things – certain types of people, places, situations, sights, sounds, smells, and so on. We have accumulated impressions from the past, and when we encounter a similar impression in the present, we feel attracted towards the object that is the source of it. It is almost as though we need a kind of 'fix'. If we do not get it from time to time, we feel inner dissatisfaction.

Based on such experiences we come to believe that the only way we can access pleasurable feelings is through these objects, and so we try to intensify and solidify our relationship to them. When there is need, dependency is already forming. We begin to rely on that person, situation or item in order to get in touch with this pleasurable feeling. Pleasure easily becomes pain through this dependency, whether it's in the form of a cigarette, making love or the need for approval. Buddhist parents will tell their children that the best doctors are Dr Awareness, Dr Inner Peace and Dr Wisdom.

Although our feeling of pleasure may have arisen out of contact with an external object, we must ask ourselves whether that object is necessary in order to feel happy. There can be a deepening of happiness when there is less dependence on external factors. Meditation has an important part to play. As our meditation deepens and we discover inner contentment, we reduce our reliance on external factors significantly. Reducing such dependency takes pressure off our mind. It creates an opportunity for natural warmth and contact with the world. We experience a spacious quality in our relationships.

We remain alert to the circles we move in. We offer and receive affection and we remain mindful. People influence us – for better or worse. We influence them in the same way. Meditation creates the space within that enables us to understand the dynamics of our interactions with others. Through inner peace, we establish a clear connection with the people we meet.

There are times when action matters more than association with the pleasant. For example, you are a parent with a young baby. It is warm and pleasant in bed on a cold winter's night. The heating is turned off. The last thing you want to do in the middle of the night is to get out of bed. Then the baby wakes up and begins to cry, which helps lessen our attachment to our own comfort. The pleasant experience of feeling warm and cosy in bed takes second place to the priority of giving love and attention to the baby. You may have to spend an hour or two walking up and down the hallway with the baby wrapped in a blanket until it settles down again.

The pursuit of the pleasant should never be a priority in life. If we spend our life constantly going for what we like, we find ourselves trapped in the cycle of satisfaction/dissatisfaction. We need to explore our infatuation with the pursuit of pleasure, the consequences of making this our priority, and how to release ourselves from it. We pay a price for the constant demands we make on others and the environment as we try to secure whatever we want for ourselves.

We can know a natural happiness and joy in daily life that has nothing to do with money, goods or getting attention from others.

# Happiness

*We may have to change our priorities and simplify our life
in order to heighten our sense of authenticity and commitment
to deeper values.*

If we are totally honest with ourselves, our motivation for whatever we do is to secure happiness and avoid unhappiness. We find a certain amount of happiness in getting the things we want. No doubt we have met, from time to time, extraordinarily happy people who possess very little, yet radiate joy. You may well ask yourself, why is it that I have so much and yet I am not happy? This materialistic age deserves to end since it fails to deliver happiness. Serving our own desires is the greatest slavery.

We have confused the message of what to buy with how to live. Once we have taken care of our basic economic needs, what surely follows is the science of life and our existence in it. We know from our own experience that acquisitions cannot provide what we truly seek. For some, however, this simple truth is recognised too late.

A woman worked as a lawyer in the city and rented an expensive flat. Her opportunities in the law firm were promising so she decided to put together a deposit and take out a mortgage to buy herself a flat. Nobody forced her into making the decision, but she thought why keep giving money away to a property owner? However, she knew the mortgage would tie her to working every available hour, and would also mean that she would need to take care she said and did nothing that might jeopardise her chances for promotion.

During a retreat, she realised that she was in debt to her bank for the next twenty-five years. 'This is a modern form of bonded labour. I am trapped, imprisoned in a system along with millions of others. I have no choice but to work the daily treadmill. Sometimes

I think I would like to use my training in law to serve the poor and the marginalised, but I can't. The salary would not even cover my monthly mortgage, let alone all my other expenses. I have to stay in the corporate world.'

It is extraordinarily difficult to deliberately lower our standard of living. It takes courage to go from a spacious flat in a well-to-do area to a cheaper place somewhere else. Single women also have to view a potential home from the standpoint of personal safety. There will always be risks, even if we truly wish to find ways to live a free and compassionate life. Lean liberty is preferable to fat slavery.

We may have to change our priorities and simplify our life in order to heighten our sense of authenticity and commitment to deeper values. Even if we take such evolutionary steps, there is no guarantee this will increase our quota of happiness. Perhaps the key is to focus on service to others instead of constantly taking for ourselves. In this way, the notion of ownership dissipates. People who experience daily life free from self-indulgence can find an abundance of natural happiness. True happiness does not depend upon the self getting what it wants.

We need surprisingly little for real happiness, as can be seen from an international survey that found the people of Bangladesh were the happiest. Such a survey deserves to trigger a flood of wealthy Western visitors to Bangladesh. Then they can find out why there is more happiness in Bangladesh than in Birmingham, Berlin or Boston. We hardly recognise the cost of an existence spent in sustaining self-interest: it is simply not possible to be happy in such circumstances. At best, we might enjoy some superficial pleasures, like living in an expensive flat.

Where there is wisdom there is happiness. In the desire to possess this and that, we turn our back on the rest of the universe. The supreme happiness is to see everything but not want to possess it. The trees, the flowers, the sunset all help to reveal your own natural happiness. Happiness is your true nature. Be happy.

# LIVING IN
# FREEDOM

*Authentic freedom, as distinct from the rhetoric of politicians,
generates love and compassion. This is what knowing the nature
of things means.*

Pride is the flower that grows in the devil's garden. The political
leaders of the West, and too many of its citizens, like to boast of
'living in freedom'. As with all conceited claims, this shows a blind
spot. It would probably be equally appropriate to describe many of
us as having a life far from freedom. For example, the USA has
imprisoned more of its citizens than any other country. One in
every 163 people in the USA is locked up. Some of these jails are
hellish places, incarcerating some of the most violent people on
earth, who inflict terrible suffering on their fellow inmates.

Many of the young, poor, sick, elderly and unemployed in the
West may also justifiably feel imprisoned by their circumstances.
They have enormous pressures exerted on them, and are then
mostly left to get on with life regardless of their personal circumstances. The 'freedom' of Western rhetoric lacks love and compassion for all; it lacks an understanding of the human condition and
that we are all related to everyone and everything else. We keep
reiterating the message of freedom when it ought to be clear to us
that far too many people feel trapped by their circumstances and
cannot see a way out.

This harsh reality of an imprisoned life is also true of the privileged. Wealth and poverty are twin sisters. There are the rich and
shameless who live imprisoned in opulence, afraid to go out in case
they are pursued and harassed. Millions of people hesitate to go out
on the streets at night in case they are mugged or worse. There are

those addicted to alcohol, drugs, gambling, money, power and sex. There are those who are unhappy, fearful and neurotic, with unresolved emotional problems. There are those who are obese, frail, stricken with ill health. There are those who hate themselves, who hurt themselves and who feel lonely and unwanted. Others are work obsessed: stressed out, moody and intolerant.

Why aren't we free? What affects us so powerfully that it can stop us from having any sense of genuine freedom at all? Perhaps if we face up to the fact that we are unfree, we can begin the journey to freedom. We need to start admitting to ourselves that the reality and the rhetoric are opposed to each other. We need to ignore the ideological ramblings of our leaders so that we can concentrate on the levels of suffering in society, and the means to resolve this suffering.

We can start to replace the ideology of individualism, profit and efficiency with community, right livelihood and skilful means. This would mean judging our standard of living by different criteria. We would not sit idly neglecting those who suffer. Our heart would have no appetite for luxury goods, not would we envy people who are possessed by their affluence. Those who express envy are indirectly admitting that they feel inferior. When selfish desire comes in through the door, love for others goes out the window.

Why do we support ideological beliefs that serve no one's true interests? Why do we do that to ourselves? We spend a large percentage of our lives trying to achieve our goals. If we were to take much less interest in our personal goals, it might awaken us to a wider vision.

There is a radically different way of looking at freedom. It is not based on self-interest but on awakening. Awakening reveals that life is so free it allows everything. Our inner life cannot inherently block freedom: it confirms it. We realise freedom is unstoppable. The sheer magnificence of the diversity of life is immediate confirmation of ultimate freedom. We are it – and we can know it. Even when unwelcome and unwanted things happen, we can acknowledge the presence of freedom in the nature of things. Ultimate and unstoppable freedom makes everything possible. Authentic freedom, as distinct from the rhetoric of politicians, generates love and compassion. This is what knowing the nature of things means.

Life is innately free: its freedom is revealed equally everywhere. It is not something that belongs to one particular nation more than another. We all have the opportunity to experience this immeasurable freedom. It is not something confined to a special environment. In this respect, freedom is available to the countless numbers incarcerated in prison as much as to the monk in a monastery in the East. To know that one abides in the Land of the Unfree may mark the first stepping stone to discovering the Land of the Free.

# DROPPING OUT

*I believe it is important that we protect people's right
to drop out to explore a different way of life. There
is a suffocating conformity in society, and it is
far better to drop out than sell out.*

There is a 2,500-year-old story of a young man in India brought up as a wealthy Brahmin. Being dissatisfied with the life that his parents had planned for him – education, courtship, marriage, inheritance of father's business – he found himself in conflict with them. His parents could not understand why their son had decided on a different way of life. They believed in the stages of life in the Brahminical traditions, which include fulfilling your obligations to family and society before retiring late in life to an ashram for meditation. The young man listened to their protest but his heart told him he had to find his own way. His reply to his parents was significant. He said, 'This world is tied to craving and clinging. I don't want to live like that.'

I meet many people who share the same view as that young man. They have deliberately turned their back on a way of life that pursues pleasure, money and status. They see the futility of it. They know that in the larger picture those caught up in this modern expression of the hunter-gatherer ideology live an irresponsible life. Such a view does not please mainstream thinking, whether such thinkers are rich or poor – they can all be remarkably intolerant of those who question their values. I have listened to the stories of some disillusioned people who have ended up on the receiving end of the wrath of others who conform.

In the late 1960s and early 1970s the message that came from some of the high priests of the hippy movement was, 'Tune in, turn on and drop out.' It was usually and deliberately associated with soft drugs and psychedelics, which seemed to be the only means available at that time to alter consciousness. Yet the message of dropping out still matters. It still needs to be shouted out across the rooftops of suburbia. People who drop out pose a threat. The most frequent charge levelled at those who drop out is that they are escaping from responsibility. We can almost hear the voices of conformists: 'What if we were all to drop out. Where would society be then?'

I believe it is important that we protect people's right to drop out to explore a different way of life. There is a suffocating conformity in society, and it is far better to drop out than sell out. Dropping out isn't easy. We can wisely escape from one numbing form of existence only to find that we have walked straight into a whole new set of challenges, for which we may feel inadequately prepared. It takes faith to maintain the integrity of such a decision: it's not easy.

We want to live with clarity, but feel under pressure from our circumstances. We feel that if only those circumstances were different, we could lead a good life. This is a rationalisation: we are avoiding the choices we do have, and this kind of realisation is questionable because it sustains the fragmentation of the individual. Our level of dissatisfaction with our circumstances increases, yet we lack the determination to make the leap from the known into the unknown.

We end up feeling worse off than our neighbours. On the surface they seem content with their lot, while we feel discontent at every level of our being. We find ourselves rejecting our daily existence and imagining an ideal one instead. Envy discourages us from looking fully at what is happening in our lives right now. It is better to look clearly and directly at how things actually are than to join the rat race.

We can feel a lot of ill will when those who are important to us hurl insults at us for refusing to conform to their way of life. People who drop out become scapegoats. They threaten the straitlaced view of things, and express different perceptions that upset the accepted worldview. It is not an easy thing to struggle daily for meaningful change as an expression of our inner freedom. Difficulties, unrest and dissatisfaction belong to a mind in which reality and ideal are divorced from each other. This is all too human. Nevertheless, we have the potential to marry ideal to reality without disappointment.

We may not always understand those who drop out, and it would be foolish if we rushed to judgement. Taken in the right spirit, such people may contribute to our awakening. It is a noble thing to refuse to identify with accepted social models. It might mean following your heart, learning to trust in life from one day to the next, and accepting the discomforts and hassles that go with change. It is worth putting up with anything to know the taste of liberation.

# WAYS OF
# RESPONDING

*You may believe that everybody acts for themselves, even if they appear to be doing things for others. Such people just want to feel good about themselves, you say.*

Every human being engages in daily activity, starting with getting out of bed in the morning. However, you need to look at *how* you act, and ask yourself what motivates you. Are you acting from self-interest, or for the benefit of others? To any question, there are only four ways of responding:

1. 'Yes'.
2. 'No'.
3. Both 'Yes' and 'No'.
4. Don't know (neither 'Yes' nor 'No').

Each response is valid assuming you speak from the truth of your experience and current understanding. You ought to be clear about these four ways of responding inwardly, even if you choose to remain silent in the face of questions.

You may conclude that the force of self-interest easily becomes the governing force for your actions. You may believe that everybody acts for themselves, even if they appear to be doing things for others. Such people just want to feel good about themselves, you say. The hardening of this view becomes cynicism, and may say more about your attitude than being an accurate comment on others. Is self-interest worthwhile in the short or long term? You may say 'yes' without any shred of doubt. If so, you may need to ask your family and friends what the consequences of your exclusive self-interest are.

If you say 'no', you may need to examine your daily life to see whether the hours you spend serving others match your response. It is important to be clear about who benefits and in what way. Sometimes the benefit or potential benefit to others is obvious. There are other times when you think your actions benefit another in the short or long term, but you may be wrong. You may cause harm. A parent smacks a child, for example, or a political leader identifies with his country. Both parent and leader imagine what they do is not for themselves but for the good of others, but they may well be deluding themselves.

If your answer is 'both yes and no', you will need to look into yourself to see specifically where you act for others and where you act for yourself. There are plenty of occasions where people's motives are mixed. It takes reflection to distinguish what is in it for you and what is for others.

Finally, the 'don't knows'. What happens to you when you experience this response? You may experience not knowing as a bare fact and have the capacity to stay steady with it. Alternatively, you may find you experience much agitation and self-doubt as a result of not knowing what to do. This indicates a resistance to the fact that you do not know. Instead of being steady with the fact and responding wisely to it, you corrupt your natural sense of worth and end up unhappy.

It would be rare for a person not to get some measure of personal satisfaction from serving others. You will feel justifiably good inside about what you have done. This is one of the natural benefits of serving others, but if you act for others solely in order to feel good about yourself, it is unlikely that you will have the power to sustain long-term service to others. In time, it will become clear whether your actions mostly serve your personal needs or not. You can't hide your underlying attitude from yourself or others. When self is centre stage, you find you keep talking about yourself, wanting praise from others, and wanting to repeat the feel-good factor. You may also feel the need to put down others engaged in similar work. The philosophy of self-interest feeds into every dynamic of daily life.

I am not advocating swinging to the other extreme and becoming a do-gooder, but instead exploring the middle ground between these two extremes of self and other. This involves not being especially identified with any of the four positions, so that you will become aware when you are ensnared in projections about yourself and others. You will also notice the way your actions move back and forth between the two.

In the fullness of clarity, a truly expanded life becomes immediately accessible. You abide free from any prejudice in terms of the four responses: there is no clinging to any of them. In an extraordinary way, an awakened life happens by itself when we are free from the shackles of self and other. There is a breathtaking intimacy with everything. We know life without chains. Such awakening is in everybody's interest.

# THE DEPTHS OF
# EXPERIENCE

# THE SHADOW
## OF *My*

---

*The attachment to* my *dominates and controls people's
lives, generating unprecedented misery. The notion of* my
*wraps itself around the nation state, religious beliefs,
property and relationships.*

By *my* I mean anything that we believe we possess or own. We tend
to use the language of *my* as an inherent truth rather than an interpretation about the way things are. The intensification of *my* can produce a frightening possessiveness leading to violence and murder. It
often acts like a dark shadow hiding a clear relationship to the
dynamics of existence. It would be an invaluable use of our time to
reflect on *my* as a false impression that generates all sorts of problems.

Repeatedly we experience that the force of *my* arises out of
desire and possessiveness. The stronger the desire and possessiveness, the stronger the belief in and identification with *my*; it can
easily become a fixation. The attachment to *my* dominates and controls people's lives, generating unprecedented misery. The notion
of *my* wraps itself around the nation state, religious beliefs, property and relationships.

Foolishly, we have allowed this concept of *my* to have an extraordinary grip over our lives, even though it distorts numerous situations. To reflect on *my* in our thinking, speech or writing can
have far-reaching effects. It is one of the most heavily charged concepts in our language. We cherish our belief in *my*, cling to it, and
value it above every other concept. The failure to see *my* as an illusion fragments the wholeness of life and distorts all that is true and
meaningful. Every perception, view and belief becomes warped
under its pressure.

It would be easy to shrug this examination off, to claim that we cannot break out of the spell of living in the shadow of *my*. But since it matters so much to us, it is surely worthwhile to take the risk of investigating what is illusory about it.

*My* can be thought of as a shorthand for the word *misery*, which also starts with an *m* and ends with a *y*. We are afraid that if we are not possessive and gripping, claiming *my* – *my* things, *my* relationship, *my* career, *my* meditation, *my* space – other people will walk all over us. In an awakened life, we acknowledge and respect what we have access to, but are free from possessiveness.

Most people try to extract a part of the world in order to feel safe and secure. We might call it *my home*. As the notion of *my* grows, it can create further fear and insecurity. For example, people find themselves afraid of intruders. 'My home is my castle,' we claim. It is hard for us to understand that if *my* loses its substance, then fear and clinging loses its grip over us as well. We will still act mindfully, taking care of our home, locking the doors and sleeping well at night. We are not afraid of losing it. We are certainly not paranoid when someone knocks on the door.

Fear is bound up in *my*, and in abandoning *my* we find we live centred and grounded in the midst of daily life. We cease to be afraid of unexpected circumstances. Suffering arises not because of what happens to us, but because we infect our sense of *my* with clinging and attachments. As we come out of our fixation, we see the emptiness and lack of substance in such possessiveness. This allows our innate affection and sensitivity to the world to express itself.

If we probe deeply and mercilessly into the effect of the sense of *my* in our lives, looking at how it distorts clear perceptions, we will cease to cling to ways of life that intensify our desire for personal security. Questioning this manifestation of ego, we can examine the fiction that something or someone belongs to us as a possession. The use of the word *my* then becomes simply a convention. It does not stand as a reference. True reality stands alone and free from illusions of *my* and *mine*. Seeing and understanding the illusion of *my* sets us free.

# GLIMPSES

*It may be that we feel unable to make sense of certain
experiences despite our quiet efforts to understand them.
There may be a profound glimpse of something, but we
feel inadequate to make complete sense of it.*

When we glimpse an insight into ourselves in meditation, or notice
something beautiful in everyday life, we only see it for a fleeting
moment before we move on to something else. We have a tendency
to allow our attention to fade: the thought comes, 'Oh, now I have
seen that, what's next?' and we stop seeing. We can't sustain that
glimpse. But isn't there more to see?

The same thing happens as we glimpse the games we play when
we experience emotional difficulties. A voice within knows that our
dramas are not such a big drama. These insights provide marvellous opportunities for a direct link to our deep, clear inner knowing, but few people are willing to acknowledge them. As we glimpse
the insubstantiality of our soap opera, its structure is weakened.
Those glimpses, that direct seeing, are the inner revolution that can
bring our mind games to a halt.

How can meditation, with its form, structure and emphasis on
the inner world, lead us towards greater awareness in the outer
world? It is by practising meditation that we develop a willingness
to see directly into the whole field of our inner life. Looking with
genuine openness, we learn to see the deeper levels of our mind
more clearly. Wise fish swim near the seabed. We glimpse the factors that influence our personality. We learn to cultivate the
healthy and overcome the unhealthy.

Most of us probably underestimate the importance of these
glimpses that touch us so deeply. We acknowledge the experience
rather than take an interest in the insight. What does the glimpse

tell us? What is to be discovered? What does it say about the self, control and choice? What is revealed about what matters and what does not matter? There is no need to fix experiences into a single frame, since we can value them for the insights they provide and what they point to.

It may be that we feel unable to make sense of certain experiences despite our quiet efforts to understand them. There may be a profound glimpse of something, but we feel inadequate to make complete sense of it. At such times, it is worthwhile making contact with someone who understands the field of experience, spiritual and otherwise. Such a person may be able to suggest the significance of such glimpses, although some glimpses cannot be explained by anyone. Deep experiences carry their own authority.

We can sustain them through the power of bare attention to an object, a skill that is developed through meditation. For example, we can meditate on a poem and suddenly glimpse a deep truth that the poet is pointing to. Meditation allows us to live more fully in our inner lives and, equally important, makes a most significant contribution to the depths of experience that can shake up our conditioned view of things. It is one of the most important resources available to humanity and sadly one of the most neglected.

If we are focused and receptive, we can become a vehicle for illumination, and turn our attention towards what we know in our hearts it is necessary to see. With awareness, interest and presence, we can uncover what has previously been covered. The world has much to reveal to us, provided we are willing to make ourselves receptive to it. We can discover a larger sense of life that places our personal circumstances into a different dimension altogether.

There are times when our own personal story matters little and we sense something other that is inexplicable. In this sense of wonder we love witnessing the stars at night, a beautiful face, a flower, a bird flying through the air, or the dynamics of city life. We sense the possibility for abiding effortlessly and freely in something vast.

# THE REWARD

*Our job becomes increasingly meaningless, petty and tedious*
*when money is the only reward. There's a real sadness in having*
*to live like that: life becomes a dreadful drudgery.*

You have probably at some time said to yourself, 'What made me do that? Why on earth did I do that? What got into me?' This kind of reaction shows we lack understanding of our own psychological processes. We have not looked sufficiently at ourselves. For example, we say something vicious or hurtful. We have done something that can only be described in the kindest possible way as inappropriate, and which gets us into an awful lot of trouble. It might produce guilt, denial or despair from within, and invite personal attack from others.

What becomes apparent is how much a single error of judgement can affect what we do. It is not easy to accept what we have brought upon ourselves through the decisions we have made. We need to examine our actions. We need to have the capacity to stop and examine what is driving us on. We need to be willing to pull out of a situation if we sense it is going to end in disappointment. For example, we don't like work. We don't like going to work. The day seems endless and we can't wait to finish work and get away. Work is viewed solely for one purpose – to make money. The more money we make and the quicker we make it the better off we feel.

Consequently, we look forward to Friday night or the end of the month when our pay packet comes. We look forward to our three or four weeks' holiday a year. Our job becomes increasingly meaningless, petty and tedious when money is the only reward. There's a real sadness in having to live like that: life becomes a dreadful drudgery. Are there other work options open to us? The

71

primary feature of our mind, rolling on from one day to the next, becomes dissatisfaction. It makes us indifferent and lazy.

One man, who lived in a town with high unemployment, was fortunate to have a job. He worked forty hours a week, plus a few hours a week overtime. From time to time he felt grateful for the opportunity to work, but that became increasingly rare. For the most part, he hated the job. He had just turned thirty, and kept wondering to himself what had happened to all the promises of youth. He didn't feel particularly ambitious. He didn't think those further up the corporate ladder had a better quality of life than he did. Most of the conversations he engaged in in and out of the office seemed banal.

He found himself getting more irritable, and sometimes mild feelings of depression descended on him. He said he had read the story of the Buddha, who fled his responsibilities at the same age, yet he couldn't imagine himself doing the same thing, although he had neither wife nor children. It may be necessary to step out of our old life just as a snake leaves behind its old and worn-out skin. We may say, wisely, that 'money doesn't bring happiness', but unfortunately we don't believe what we say. We spend our days fretting over our financial circumstances, moaning about bank charges and credit card bills. Such complaints leave us feeling poor and possibly envying those who seem rich.

We forget that the rich often don't feel rich. They enter grandiose schemes to make even more money. They will even risk the substantial amounts that they have already in their determination to make even more money. It's hard to imagine when we struggle along to make ends meet on a modest salary. We have to stop, reflect on what we have already, and find contentment even in the face of genuine financial hardship.

There is enough light within us to shine into every area of our life, even our finances. If we fail to make use of this light, we will spend our life living in darkness, never happy in ourselves or with others. We do not have to live in a gloomy way around work and money. When our light shines in the darkness, the darkness disappears. We can see in ways that we have never seen before. There is no greater blessing than knowing this through direct experience. No wonder the wise live happily in this world.

# DEEP TIME

*We practise being conscious and alert to what is present in this moment, no matter what the task. Communication matters immensely, so we practise speaking what is both true and useful.*

I know a couple who have been married for several years. Like many other couples, they lead full lives, yet they also need to give time to their marriage. They used to find that they would forget to mention little things – good and bad – that struck them about each other. Upsets built up. This became a pattern that at times left both of them feeling somewhat at a distance from each other. One day they sat down together and talked about the difficulty they had in living together and yet at times feeling distant from each other.

They decided to set an hour aside each week for what they called 'deep time', designed to give them the opportunity to catch up with each other. They told each other the warm and kind things they had noticed that had gone unsaid. They also mentioned situations that had made them irritated. The couple told me how much they appreciated 'deep time'. They felt closer to each other.

When we are not aware and lack care in our relationships, we find we succumb to the driving forces of the mind. It is as though we are swept away by a fast-flowing river. Part of the problem is that we have such little real regard for the present moment. Our mind runs up and down between past, present, and future, dwelling on fantasies and daydreams. Living our daily life in this way weakens the very structure of our mind, making us prone to anxiety and agitation.

We get used to living like this and hardly question our state of mind. We don't even imagine that we can respond to situations in daily life in a different way. Wisely, the Buddhist tradition has given much greater priority to full awareness here and now than to faith. It states that mindfulness acts as one of the best supports for a stable and clear mind. The Buddha gave a famous talk on the foundations of mindfulness, in which he said a practitioner of his teachings:

> Acts in full awareness when looking ahead and looking away. Acts in full awareness when flexing and extending his limbs . . . Acts in full awareness when eating, drinking, consuming food and tasting . . . Acts in full awareness when defecating and urinating. Acts in full awareness walking, standing, sitting, falling asleep, waking up, talking and keeping silent . . . and abides independent and free from clinging to anything in the world.

These words remind all of us to pay real attention to what occurs in the present moment. In the Buddhist tradition, formal meditation includes training and developing the mind to be grounded and centred from one moment to the next. If our mind is not in good order, then nothing appears right. As our mind becomes clear, bright and stable through the training of full awareness meditation on the here and now, everything else finds itself clearly revealed like a reflection in a bright mirror.

We practise being conscious and alert to what is present in this moment, no matter what the task. Communication matters immensely, so we practise speaking what is both true and useful. When things go unsaid, it makes us feel uncomfortable. When another also says little, we tend to start interpreting in our own way. Through cultivating mindfulness, we establish a factual relationship with what is actually happening in the present. Then there is the opportunity to respond wisely to the immediate situation. 'Deep time' needs to be a frequent feature of our lives.

Being mindful of the present situation contributes to integrating our human condition. The present is here regardless of whether you and I are in touch with it or not. The present is also here regardless of any views and opinions we might have about it. This moment is all we have: anything else is an abstraction. Anything else is an image or an idea. Life is here in this moment, and this moment serves as a key to awakening.

# SIGNS OF CHANGE

*We may have made a nice job, nice home and nice partner our top priority, but they cannot act as a substitute for awakening, teachings and spiritual community.*

He came to the retreat during a period of major transition in his life. His relationship of several years had ended. He had just resigned from being an accountant for years. He was fed up with dealing with numbers for a soulless company in the city. The lease had run out on his flat. To cap it all, he had read in a national newspaper that finding a job, moving home and ending a relationship constitute the three primary causes of stress. All three were happening to him at the same time. In good moments, he told me, he could smile at his current circumstances.

Sometimes he woke up in the morning elated. No job. No woman in his bed. Soon, no bed. It was a time of transition, full of opportunity. Other days he woke up feeling very low. It was hard enough to cope with one thing at a time, let alone all three at once. In such times, he would pull the bedclothes over his head and try to go back to sleep. His friends were not much use, and kept giving him different advice. Then he picked up a book (Jack Kornfield's *A Path with Heart*) in a bookshop. At the back, it contained the address of Gaia House retreat centre. He went off to sit a retreat without having a clue what use it might be.

He felt this pressure in his chest. 'I feel my heart just wants to break free,' he told me. 'Then I start thinking about all these decisions I have to make. Then I start to contract.' Sometimes he looked heavy with the world and sometimes his eyes revealed happiness and a determination to open up his life. At the end of the retreat, he made a decision. A few months later, I saw him again when he came to participate in two retreats in Bodh Gaya in

India. He had new priorities more significant than job, home and lover.

To their credit, a growing number of people wish to make the switch from a materialistic life to exploring a meaningful lifestyle. They listen to a voice from within that calls for change, for risk and service to others rather than the pursuit of a self-centred career. There are many good-hearted people around who have no wish to climb on the backs of others in a pursuit of power and profit.

The ego always falls short of awakening the heart and becomes satisfied with lesser attainments. We may have made a nice job, nice home and nice partner our top priority, but they cannot act as a substitute for awakening, teachings and spiritual community. We sell ourselves short when we opt for less than enlightenment. We see the ego finds security in possessions, but becomes dependent on the notion of possession for its very survival.

The grasping ego corrupts the mind, and directly or indirectly our relationship with others and ourselves. A regular dissatisfaction and a feeling of pressure on your chest are like sympathetic signals that it is time for a change, either in attitude or activity. There is something wonderful about opening our heart and feeling that we are doing something worthwhile. Deep experience brings light into our lives, enabling us to leave behind the limited and unfulfilling. Many people have stories of times of transition. We can look back over our lives to times when we knew we had to make a switch. This meant no going back to the old: no more continuity of an unfulfilling lifestyle. It is one thing to experience a way of life that seems at a deep level rather pointless. It is something else to follow our heart and know, deep down, that something is purposeful and appropriate.

If our deep experiences fail to cause us to leave selfish tendencies behind, they end up feeding the ego rather than dissolving it. Pride and conceit set in. We get caught up in feeling superior, different from others. Everybody wants to feel special and unique. We tell ourselves that we are, and we want others to tell us so as well. Wise people stop clinging to experiences to sustain the continuity of the ego. Left with nothing whatsoever to feed on, the ego feels powerless. Then the ego withers away, and what is profound is left.

# WHAT IS
# THE COST?

*When we realise the emptiness of personal wealth,*
*we have a duty to change our lifestyle and find our*
*freedom as a human being.*

In most areas of our life, if we decide we really want something (within reason, of course), we can succeed. To succeed, we have to put together certain factors, including ambition, energy, discipline, knowledge and resources. Then we can get what we want. If we push and shove our way towards our ends, the chances are that we will eventually arrive there, or feel an utter failure. If we don't work towards our goals, we can end up feeling that we are wasting our life.

One of the questions that we need to ask ourselves regularly is: 'What is the cost of an unexamined life?' It would be a pity to look back over the years and feel that we had missed various opportunities. It's easy to lose our capacity for looking at things in an independent way. At times, we might be left asking ourselves if other people can do it, why can't I?

I met a rather spirited woman some time ago whose husband worked in international business. She told me he had worked his way up the corporate ladder and now earned more than half a million dollars a year. She had ended up living in eight or more different places. He was a 'company man', and one of the difficulties of such a lifestyle is keeping such people's partners entertained, so, for example, his company arranged a diamonds-and-furs auction for the wives of the company directors. The woman told me that one day, talking on the phone to another company wife, she had blurted out, 'I hate the company. I hate this way of life. I hate the superficiality of it all.' To her surprise, her friend agreed with her but was afraid to talk about it. The woman went to her husband and said, 'I can't go on living like this.' He became angry and couldn't understand how she could be so ungrateful after all he had done for her. He suggested that she see a psychoanalyst. A few months later, she left him and moved to a one-bedroom apartment in another city, where she started learning yoga and meditation, and working in a low-income office job. She said to me, 'I've never been so happy in all my life.' One who has enough is content with little.

Despite propaganda from governments and the corporate world, wealth generates its own problems. When we realise the emptiness of personal wealth, we have a duty to change our lifestyle and find our freedom as a human being. Money can ease a situation but it will not make you happy. Those who trust rotten boughs may fall.

Many of us carry around with us every day the feeling that we are poor, and the desire to be better off. There is no chance of any peace of mind while we live like this.

When we refuse to subscribe to the world of diamonds and furs, we can participate fully in the real world of suffering and the joy of transformation. Transformation is available for those who are willing to take risks, and for that we need each other. It was the woman's telephone conversation with her friend that gave her the impetus to move out.

We need support for freedom, inquiry and discovery. We need to listen to the voices of the wise and free. Sometimes they're living next door to us and we don't even realise it. Sometimes they are not, for our leafy suburb may house only other equally imprisoned minds.

# WILLING TO STOP

*In non-doing and inner stillness, we experience a wealth of nourishment. Out of non-doing comes meaningful activity. Such an experience acts as the springboard for wise engagement with this world.*

In some respects, meditation is the art of doing as little as possible. The moment we stop doing, all manner of inner states of mind may surface – a wandering mind, a thinking mind, fears, agitation, a desire to be self-important. Can we give ourselves this opportunity to be still, to know inner silence? It is essential to remain patient with the unsatisfactory movements of our inner life, and not to latch on to them; not to use them to measure ourselves, others, or life itself. Stillness is the mother of wisdom.

When we first engage in formal sitting meditation, we think we should be quiet and still within, but we may experience an upsurge of commotion. This restlessness and inner chatter is the normal background to our existence that has now become the foreground. The unconscious is becoming conscious. Our noisy and restless mind influences, informs, and shapes our way of life.

The mind is a vast dimension, as deep and extensive as the world that we look out upon. So the mind can embrace and accommodate any contradiction in life – the beautiful and the ugly, right and wrong, positive and negative. When we explore the internal universe, we can find space to attend to any unexamined areas in our way of living, and this space within has significance for every one of us.

To stop being pushed along by pressure, thought, reaction and habit, we must be willing to stop ourselves, and be still. Meditation points to a deep stillness in the midst of life. We can then appreciate the majesty of the earth and the wondrous diversity of sentient life. In non-doing and inner stillness, we experience a wealth of nourishment. Out of non-doing comes meaningful activity. Such an experience acts as the springboard for wise engagement with this world.

The true actions of life come from non-doing. From the ground of non-doing, everything happens mystically and magically. Enlightenment becomes available to all of us, not just to the privileged few living a saintly life. Non-doing is alien to our culture, however, so we often reject it. Yet we experience moments of appreciation for non-doing. We know the feeling of relief when we complete a task; of delight when we have nothing to do; of contentment when we are making no demands upon the world. There is much to realise in non-doing.

The sages of the East coined the term 'actionless action'. The ordinary mind might think that such a term is nonsense, but the wise know its significance.

# WISE SPEECH

*Our values and priorities are revealed through speech. In our day-to-day circumstances, we need to endeavour to be watchful of everything that comes out of our mouth. That is our vigilance.*

Words seem to have a remarkable power. They are nothing of themselves, only what we make of them, but we have become bewitched with words. Every year we have access to more and more concepts. There are more and more things to talk about, more and more books to read. We have become eloquent. We like to express ourselves well and feel that we have a command over the language. As a result, we are easily impressed with those who use language in a sophisticated way.

There are countless authorities on every imaginable subject. No matter how much we know, it seems to be only the tip of the iceberg of information available. We need to think again about our enchantment with words and its manifestation in thoughts, speech and writing. The language that we use tells us something about ourselves but does not necessarily reveal clarity, integrity and wisdom.

I remember, as a young reporter in the mid 1960s, attending various government press conferences. We would listen to a minister's spokesperson. Reporters would ask all the right questions but never seem to get a straight answer. We would sit there dutifully putting pen to paper, knowing deep within that there was collective deceit taking place. It is a strange climate to experience. We felt that we were not told lies and we were not told the truth either.

I believe that this is a common experience for television viewers or radio listeners interested in political programmes. In Dharma teachings, clarity means engaging in communication free from deceit on behalf of a cause. We easily confuse the capacity to articulate views and opinions as expressions of clarity. I remember the spokespersons appeared very knowledgeable, handled the persistent questions of the media with deft ability, and were rarely stumped for an answer. Their body language expressed a statesmanlike authority and they sounded confident and well briefed. But as we listened, we felt an unease inside. There was a sense that the government spokesperson was either being incredibly economical with the truth or simply had no mind of his or her own. Things haven't changed.

Our values and priorities are revealed through speech. In our day-to-day circumstances, we need to endeavour to be watchful of everything that comes out of our mouth. That is our vigilance. The key to wise speech is watching what we say and its impact upon others. Backbiting, slander, patronising and arrogant speech reveal an unhealthy self. The practice of wise speech includes refusing to feed malicious and cynical conversations, regardless of what anybody says. We can easily conform to the complaining mind that runs through our culture, and there is a terrible tendency for our mind to get stuck in particular points of view. What comes out of our mouth will often reveal more about ourselves than what we are talking about.

Sometimes we need to observe noble silence rather than engage in ignoble speech. This may upset other people. They may accuse us of being aloof, but we know we mean well. It is not easy to stay detached from crude judgements, but there is a long-standing tradition of observing noble silence in the face of accusations, lies and hypocrisy. Two thousand years ago, the rabbi from Nazareth observed noble silence, even when asked by a powerful political leader what the truth was. The rabbi knew better than to sink to the level of debate with his tormentors.

As we develop inwardly, we begin to talk about things differently. There is a wisdom and kindness to what we say. We are less judgemental and show a more thoughtful attitude towards circumstances. Right speech is a tremendous challenge, and sometimes it seems much easier to fall in with the superficiality of conversations rather than appear different. We often think that what we say to another is for their ears only, even if we don't make that clear at the time. We forget that what is whispered in an ear is often heard a hundred miles away.

This does not mean that we become terribly serious and only talk about deep matters. Joy, good humour and common sense are also fruits of wise speech. Undertaking the practice of wise speech is a true act of kindness. Since the things we say often travel much further afield than we realise, we need to stick to the principle that whatever we say about someone who is not present, we would be willing to say in the same way, in the same tone, to their face. If not, it is preferable to observe noble silence: when there are no hearers there are no recriminations later.

When we were children, we learnt the lines: 'Sticks and stones may break my bones but words can never hurt me.' If only that was true. What people say about us can hurt, and people do say things to hurt others. That is their intention. People bully, humiliate and threaten others through their words. These are acts of emotional cruelty. When we latch on to words, they can sink deep into our feelings, making us feel distressed and wounded no matter how brave a face we put on.

Yet they are only words. No more, no less. It takes equanimity to stay steady in the face of words. We have one ear for praise and another ear for blame, so let us practise staying centred between our two ears.

# THE VULNERABILITY
# OF KINDNESS

*We may not feel any sympathy for their values and decisions, but
we do not have to build a wall of resistance against them. Let's
never forget that our blood is all of one colour.*

Acts of loving kindness keep the heart open, and as we gradually
perceive this, we develop a sense of the sacredness of life. We
experience life as rare, precious, and acutely vulnerable. When we
genuinely feel this sacredness, we know the pain of that vulnerabil-
ity. Witnessing the process of birth, or watching the fading away of
life into death, shows us how tentative all forms of sentient existence are. The fragility of existence deserves daily acknowledgement so that we never take anyone or anything for granted.

A few years ago, while giving teachings in the forest in north-
ern New South Wales, Australia, I met a man who was actively
engaged in campaigns for the preservation of rainforests. With
much sadness, he related that there was a time when he loved being
in these forests and in his native Australia. He loved the diversity
of the trees, foliage and sentient life he found there. But he knew
how vulnerable forests were to vested interests. Governments, cor-
porations, logging companies and farmers destroy an acre of forest
every minute. This made him angry, and affected his capacity to
enjoy his time in these forests. I suggested that through regular lov-
ing-kindness meditation, he could again experience his love for the
rainforest on his visits – the painful information about destruction
would not corrupt his heart.

We can bring loving kindness into many features of our life.
There is something very satisfying about contributing to the happiness and security of others, although caring for the welfare of

others, including all forms of sentient life, makes us vulnerable. We might be misunderstood, overstretched, or caught up in conflict. There is enough anger in the world already, so there is little point in adding to it in the name of our ideals.

We may profoundly disagree with other people. We may not feel any sympathy for their values and decisions, but we do not have to build a wall of resistance against them. Let's never forget that our blood is all of one colour. If we believe they are truly different, we cannot act wisely in the face of fresh information. When our mind hardens, it forms a barrier to our deeper feelings. Then we may make cold, negative judgements that probably won't serve the true interests of others. Where there is kindness, we are willing to struggle with difficult decisions out of respect for others and ourselves.

Some people get the idea that living with kindness is a mistake. Kind people always get walked over, they claim, and so they harden their hearts so that nobody can reach them. That same defensive wall also stops them from reaching deep within themselves. There are risks in kindness. The most obvious one is being taken advantage of by the selfish and unscrupulous. Yes, that happens, but authentic kindness, tempered with equanimity, will not wither under such exploitation. Our kindness is then a public statement of personal dignity. Furthermore, a good conscience makes for a soft pillow.

There is a well-known saying, 'You need to be cruel to be kind'. Parents use it to justify their strictness with their children. We sometimes imagine that if we shout or yell abuse we will provoke deeper resources within a person into action. We are deceiving ourselves, however, and are likely to do more harm than good. If we sincerely wish to inspire others, we need first to know them, to respect and understand them.

The power of loving kindness is its ability to reach deep into a person, motivate them and inspire them towards greater things. It is the ability to help a person know their sense of worth and their capacities. This skill is born from awareness.

I remember going regularly to a local football match. The team struggled week after week near the foot of the division. They were in danger of being relegated – usually regarded as the worse nightmare for a club, apart from financial ruin. I stood on the terraces only a matter of five or six yards from the manager. During the match, the manager yelled abuse at several of his players. He made them all too conscious of his presence. As a result, they kept looking to him for approval, and seemed unable to get on with the game. They could not concentrate as the shadow of the manager stretched across the ground. It seemed to me to be one more example of the limitations of the force of verbal aggression, no substitute for calm skill, precise instructions and kind and firm leadership.

# ALLOWING OURSELVES TO BE TOUCHED

*These ordinary and everyday things nourish your inner being. It borders on the tragic to take the ordinary moments of daily life for granted.*

The indoors has been substituted for the outdoors. We forget we come from nature, belong to nature, and return to it. We pay a price for this loss of connection. There is a loss of intimacy and respect for land, water and air. Nature means little to us so we exploit it every conceivable way. The earth is our home yet we systematically tear it apart. Perhaps we will only know the value of water when the wells are dry.

When we turn our attention to religious texts, we notice that many of the deep experiences of the saints and sages took place outdoors. In the Buddhist tradition, monks wandered for nine months a year and spent three months a year, during the monsoon season, in one place engaged in meditation. So for much of the year they walked everywhere. They understood themselves as organic elements in vast sea of elemental life.

When I was a Buddhist monk, my teacher, Venerable Ajahn Dhammadharo, took the monks and nuns on long walks through the Thai countryside. We walked on the warm earth in a single line, silently, beneath the hot sun. There was a wonderful rhythm and a sense of harmony with everything that was around us. At night, we each hung a mosquito net over a large umbrella that hung from a tree, so we could sleep beneath the stars.

Initially, some of us were reluctant to leave the monastery to go on such walks up and down hills and across rice paddies. Instead, we wanted to stay in the monastery and continue in our meditation practice. Through these walking pilgrimages, we learnt that such walks offer something that leaves words behind. I can't explain the impact of such experiences. The benefits included a lifelong love and intimacy with everything around me. Since I disrobed, I have campaigned for environmental justice and protection. I stood for Parliament on two occasions for the Green Party. I have led back-packing retreats. I love long-distance running. I believe my years as a Buddhist monk influenced these priorities in my life.

Meditation fits well with movement and outdoor life. When we engage in movement, we love periods of stillness. When we engage in stillness, we love periods of activity. One of the purposes of meditation is to bring awareness to every step we take.

Meditation also points to intimacy with the web of life. We can ask ourselves, 'What really touches me?' We can be deeply touched in meditation from deep within and through the senses. Meditation can open the doors of perception. When there is a willingness to live mindfully, we create an opportunity for the touch of the senses to run deep inside in delightful ways. Through clarity of under-standing, we experience these joys naturally, easily, and effort-lessly. Authentic meditation makes us receptive to liberating discoveries which are unavailable to the chattering mind.

Sensing and observing the immensity of mountains, ocean or forests can touch something deep within. The dawn chorus, the sound of happy people talking together, or silence itself can touch us in an unhindered way. Smelling flowers or incense seems to bypass our conditioning and arouse a sense of mystery. Meditation develops this power to experience intimacy with the here and now.

Moments of meditation can include mindfully and slowly mov-ing your hand on the earth to experience an intimate closeness. Let your fingers feel the grass. Experience the wind brushing across your cheeks. Be receptive. Be present. Be alert. These ordinary and everyday things nourish your inner being. It borders on the tragic to take the ordinary moments of daily life for granted. These 'tremendous trifles' transcend their ordinariness when we put self-interest aside and allow the miracle of existence to touch us.

Each of our senses is a doorway to knowing the world. If our mind is like a pure, bright, clean mirror, we will know the world in a totally different way; there will be a different quality to life itself. In truth, the world is not as we *think* it to be; yet the world is not altogether otherwise.

The resolution of this paradox has the power to enlighten our life.

# BELIEFS

*We invest in our beliefs: clinging to our position becomes our reality. There is never any peace of mind when we live this way.*

Years ago, a Christian missionary called at the home of a respected Indian philosopher. The missionary carried in his hand a copy of the Bible, from which he began quoting to the philosopher. The philosopher quietly and gently pointed out that in the long tradition of Indian spirituality very similar passages were found in their sacred texts. He said that many of these passages were recorded long before Jesus walked on the earth.

The missionary became increasingly self-righteous. He quoted the most well-known passage of the Gospels, John 14:6, where Jesus says: 'I am the way, the truth, and the life: no one comes to the Father except by me.' He then told the philosopher that Hinduism, Buddhism and Islam were the tools of the Devil. He spoke with aggression and arrogance. The philosopher looked the missionary in the eye and quietly said, 'What can Jesus do for me? He doesn't seem to have done anything for you!'

We can easily confuse belief with the teachings of Jesus. Love counts, not belief. The kindly philosopher knew this very well. When we identify strongly with our beliefs, it is often at the expense of love. In the course of time, the mind develops a strong conviction about something. Holding tightly to that belief, we want to persuade others of it. We want them to believe the same things that we do. We become more and more intolerant of other beliefs, even though noticing somebody else's ego ought to remind us to work on our own. It seems particularly ironic when these beliefs involve religious feelings and matters of love.

Beliefs become a problem when they get attached to personal feelings such as pride, self-righteousness and arrogance. Instead of contributing to the happiness and peace of mind of others, we make other people's lives miserable through our beliefs. We might even imagine that they are stupid or blind. We need to look at the intention behind our beliefs, to unpack the solidification of our ego around them. We need to examine both our beliefs and any self-righteousness that accompanies them.

When we can't get our own way, we become more demanding and resentful. Our ego and set of beliefs are in conflict with someone else's and each of us wants to triumph over the other. When we believe that our beliefs matter most, we can lash out at those who dispute our position. Such situations perpetuate themselves as long as our inner life remains unexamined. We begin to feel increasingly isolated. We cannot understand why other people, except for those who hold the same beliefs, withdraw from us.

We keep justifying our position and condemning others in the vain hope that we can resolve these conflicts with other people, but we are merely fanning the flames of negativity. Shouting and arguing are evidence of warfare between two egos, each trying to defeat the other. If we can't get our way, we will lie or exaggerate circumstances to achieve supremacy. Such lies and deception increase the level of pain and hurt, but we keep trying to impose our views on others as though we alone can see the situation correctly.

People are not stupid. Most can tell when our ego is willing to say anything to gain the upper hand. It is not only that people lose their respect for us, but eventually we lose respect for ourselves. We invest in our beliefs: clinging to our position becomes our reality. There is never any peace of mind when we live this way.

It's worth being as honest and truthful as you can. In the final analysis, it is love that matters. Love needs to be the foundation for our beliefs.

# HABIT

*We always have a choice to either continue along the same old lines or explore ways to change. If it's clear to you that the old way isn't working, you should be inspired to reflect on the matter.*

We all know how difficult it is to break free from unsatisfactory habits that dominate our lives. When we are trapped in habits, we lose the capacity to be truly creative and spontaneous in our response to situations. Habits arise through repeating frequently actions that were probably initially voluntary. Our mind gets used to dealing in the same way with whatever arises in our daily life. Consequently, we neglect the importance of paying attention to the moment and making wise choices and rely upon our habits to guide us.

When we keep performing tasks in the same old way, the quality of our attention is reduced. There is a kind of motorised response that makes us think we can react more promptly to certain events. In fact, we have become imprisoned in the past. There are certain tasks that are suited to such a habitual response, but there are situations where such habits generate impulses or urges that we find difficult to overcome.

Our habits affect our feelings, thoughts and ways of looking at situations. They make a considerable contribution to the make-up of our personality. If we are to change unsatisfactory habits, we have to be clear about their strength. We may be deceiving ourselves if we think if we can overcome them through our own volition: we may need the support of other people. The habit of periodic cravings, for example, can play havoc with our lives as well as bringing about much stress and anxiety for those dear to us. It takes focused attention to a habit to be able to overcome it.

Initially, focused attention may seem to make the problem worse. In the full light of awareness, we can feel overwhelmed by the power the habit has over our lives. The will to change is vital. Since we have acquired these habits through various conditions in the past, support from others, focused attention and a daily commitment to change are invaluable resources in overcoming painful habits.

To break habits, we have to act immediately, as the resolve will weaken if we put off changing the pattern even for one day. Environment plays an important part in sustaining habits, and it is important to avoid situations that easily stimulate the habit – if you're giving up alcohol, keep away from pubs.

We always have a choice to either continue along the same old lines or explore ways to change. If it's clear to you that the old way isn't working, you should be inspired to reflect on the matter. In the process of stopping a habit, we may need to introduce positive steps so that as we struggle to overcome the old, we simultaneously develop something new that is healthy. If we give up eating junk food, we can develop an appreciation of wholesome food so that we lose the desire for food that isn't good for us.

Some habits are almost exclusively emotional. For example, somebody criticises us. This may be helpful feedback or off-the-wall and unkind comments about our work or ourselves. Our immediate response is likely to be to feel very self-conscious; to blush; or to feel guilty and become afraid of having further contact with that person. Such reactions are often habitual.

In situations like that, we have to learn to take little notice of what is taking place in our feelings and instead to listen to the bare facts. Were the comments accurate? Was it helpful? What way can the criticism be useful in the future? Was it unfair, exaggerated or untrue? We need to take notice of our mind rather than our emotions; otherwise, emotional habit in such circumstances will never change.

It is always a challenge to change unsatisfactory habits but the capacity to do so helps mould our character so that we live in clarity, comfortable with ourselves and conducting our lives with integrity. To be stuck in our habits denies a basic freedom. We will never feel good about ourselves and will also make other people's lives uncomfortable.

There is an extraordinary freedom in living without being a slave to our habits. We find the capacity to explore a wide range of interests and an enthusiasm for inquiry that stays with us throughout our whole life.

# IMPULSES

*We fail to see within, and meanwhile pressure builds up
and impulsive action becomes an escape valve.*

I was leading a retreat in a monastery in India several years ago, when I saw one of the retreatants sitting on the concrete pathway nursing a cut knee and bleeding toe. I asked him what had happened. He said that while engaged in slow, mindful walking meditation, he had suddenly felt like 'spontaneously running'. He forgot he was wearing a lungi, a long piece of white cotton cloth that is wrapped around the waist. As the retreatant took the first running step, his toe caught in the bottom of the cloth around his ankle and he flew through the air and landed on the concrete, cutting his knee and stubbing his toe. I expressed a brief condolence and asked the retreatant the difference between spontaneity and a reckless impulse. I then sent someone to get a bandage and left him to reflect on the question.

An impulse is a sudden urge registering itself in speech and bodily action bringing pleasure or pain. We become impulsive, under the influence of feelings and energy. After impulsive behaviour, we feel helplessly bound to the consequences of such an impulse. We can be subjected to impulses whatever we're doing – shopping, eating, having sex, drinking, talking, driving.

We often act on our impulses. Most of the time there are no dire consequences, but we are not always so fortunate. One impulsive act can have long-term consequences. Two colleagues shared a taxi home after the office party; she invited him in; and on impulse they had sex together. But he was married, and felt ashamed afterwards. For more than a year at work, they couldn't look each other in the eye.

Impulses involving body and mind arise and subside, but at the

95

time they are remarkably powerful, especially under the influence of the force of desire. Alcohol accelerates impulsive behaviour. It takes common sense, patience and non-attachment to allow an impulse to subside so that it loses its grip over the mind. It is no easier when the impulse arises from unpleasant feelings. Somebody has upset me, so I want to say something hurtful to get revenge. Each time I see that person anger wells up in me, along with the impulse to make a cutting remark that they will never forget.

Intense impulses can be frightening. The sudden impulse to commit a violent act against ourselves or other people, or the impulse to do something really bizarre can make us wonder what the hell is going on inside us. How has the mind found itself in such a condition? Impulses are the result of unexamined and unfulfilled desires as well as suppressed emotions. We fail to see within, and meanwhile pressure builds up and impulsive action becomes an escape valve. Professional counselling may be necessary for some people.

It is wise to restrain from any blind activity of body, speech, and mind. We fuel impulses through distorted projection on to things and people. If we learn to drop smaller impulses, we can develop the capacity to let go of the big impulses that seize our mind. Being mindful of your breathing can help to dispel an impulse as it arises.

I think of impulsive behaviour and spontaneity as being significantly different. The practice of mindfulness contributes to dissolving foolish impulses that can sow the seeds of later regret. Spontaneity emerges from a mind that is free, not weighed down with fears of approval, nor charged with ego and self-interest or cut off from emotional life. It shows itself as creativity, love, the flowering of a beautiful idea and the willingness to make sudden decisions without having to mull over all the consequences first, because you trust in an appropriate outcome. Spontaneity is the movement of awareness that responds directly to our perceptions. From a place of deep abiding within, we have the capacity to respond in spontaneous ways to the unfolding events of daily life.

# FINDING ORDER, TAKING RISKS

*We take risks to find out if a truly awakened life is possible, but there is nothing to lose, and much to discover that is sublime and accessible.*

When we observe a large amount of activity in our minds, we feel unbalanced, unsettled, unable to discern clearly, perhaps even impotent. But as we observe further, we become aware that there may be too much information in our scattered mind. Some of this is useful, valid and meaningful, but the rest has little significance.

The best thing to do when you realise your mind is scattered like this is to try and redress the balance: meditate; cut down on your information overload; focus mindfully on one activity at a time. You may need to put more order into your life through practising simple disciplines. On a day-to-day basis, try to establish a quiet and effective programme that works but is not overly ambitious. At times it will seem like two steps forward and one step back, or even the other way around, but if you remain committed to putting order into your chaotic life, you will create it, and it will generate a skilful use of your energy.

There is a middle way in all of these matters. Too much emphasis on living a balanced and ordered life will hinder us from acting adventurously. When we find harmony, we feel a sense of self-worth and contentment. Finding greater balance in our lives also reveals our areas of imbalance. The greater the balance that we have in relationship to our physical and mental world, the more we notice any fluctuations which disrupt that balance.

Wisely, the Buddhist tradition has placed a great deal of emphasis on harmony, both inner and outer. On Buddhist retreats, people meditate while sitting, standing, walking and reclining. Meals are eaten in silence and work is done mindfully, making for a long, full day of conscious living. There is a sense of balance and harmony in such meditation centres and their immediate environment. Those who live there, even for a short time, develop a discipline and focus that can carry over into their daily lives. There is much to discover in an ordered life.

One man had been practising in the Buddhist tradition for more than twenty years, paying particular attention to living wisely in daily life. He had a good job, a good family life, and sat one or two week-long retreats every year. He gave support to the local Buddhist community by being a committee member. He was reliable and regarded by his friends as a pillar of strength. He took the teachings seriously and applied them with the best of his ability to his daily life. However, whenever teachers referred to such themes as enlightenment, liberation or a fully awakened life, he felt uncomfortable. Deep down, he believed that complete enlightenment was not possible for anyone living in the West. He had convinced himself of this view, and refused to take the risk of exploring the question further. He seemed attached to the benefits of a balanced way of life.

We need to challenge all our deeply held views. We need to go beyond our comfort zone, to shake our position up. Only investigation will give us insight into situations. We have to ask ourselves, 'What does it mean to be free? What is an awakened life? What is enlightenment?' We can devote time to putting balance into our lives but this only serves as a means, not an end. Liberation relates to the greater dimension, not just the personal.

We might consider what risks we need to take to awaken our lives. Intensive retreats? Periods in solitude? Abandoning future security? Right livelihood rather than pursuit of status and money? A pilgrimage to India?

On a retreat at Gaia House, a 60-year-old man came to my room in tears. He said, 'I'm a successful businessman. I have more money than I can ever spend. Deep down, I feel I've wasted my life. I never expressed my potential to do something beautiful for others.' I told him to start today.

# TEACHER AND STUDENT

*The student needs to find a teacher who is noble, worthy, disciplined in the practice, wise and kind, and associate with them for as long as necessary.*

Do I need a teacher? The simple answer is yes. In the Eastern tradition, tremendous importance is given to the relationship between teacher and student, a type of relationship virtually unknown in our Western society. (The nearest Western equivalent is a monastery or convent, where monks and nuns receive teachings and guidance from their spiritual directors.) Unlike ordinary teachers, Buddhist teachers impart more than knowledge: they endeavour to communicate wisdom as well. Knowledge becomes wisdom when it contributes directly to understanding problems, their causes and how to solve them. It is the teacher's duty to point the way to an awakened life.

Acting the part of a good friend, a teacher directs the student towards enlightenment through embracing ethics, meditation and wisdom. Students spend time with the teacher. Their commitment includes listening to teachings, questions and answers, facing questions and applying the practices recommended by the teacher in daily life. Students must see for themselves what works in this relationship. There are different approaches that people take in being with a teacher, including:

- Having a single teacher.
- Having a main teacher and secondary teachers.
- Having several teachers.
- Associating with one or more teachers for as long as necessary

before moving on to others.

- Being independent after periods with a teacher or teachers.
- A small minority – and it's a very small one – have the inner wisdom and clarity not to need a teacher.

A teacher's authority generally comes from their teacher(s), the tradition, and their own experience. Teachers demand too much when they expect, or encourage, personal submission to themselves or their methodology. Such an attitude takes away freedom from students rather than pointing to it. Anyone in authority is vulnerable. A teacher can make one foolish mistake and hear about it a hundred times. The student needs to find a teacher who is noble, worthy, disciplined in the practice, wise and kind, and associate with them for as long as necessary.

There are a number of things that students should bear in mind in their relationship with a teacher. The first thing is a teacher accepts his or her student whereas the student is free to accept his or her teacher or not. Or a teacher may recommend a seeker to another path. There is a tendency among some students to project all manner of qualities on to a teacher, which can lead to disappointment later. To idolise a teacher, to regard him or her as a Buddha or a Christ, says more about the student than it does about the teacher.

If students ignore, or try to explain away, a teacher's questionable behaviour, the consequence to the relationship hurts both parties. Some project their negativity on to a teacher, continually finding fault with them. Some teachers seem thin-skinned, and cannot handle negativity or even criticism easily. They refute all accusations, get very defensive, and feel the need to justify themselves again and again. They throw any criticisms or ill-will back at their students, telling them that it is all in their mind.

Generally, teachers and students receive as much respect as they show. Some teachers like to think of themselves as a pure mirror of their students' experiences. They even tell their students to think of them as a Buddha, but this is very rarely true. A Buddha mind sees effortlessly the emptiness of all language. There is nothing to defend, and nothing to dismiss.

Most serious students practise stabilising meditations that enable them to pass through the agreeable and disagreeable periods with teachers. Students get to know their teachers' strengths and weaknesses. They always have the right to point things out to their teacher, since the teacher represents something noble. A teacher may make mistakes, even serious errors of judgement. Patterns will continue unless pointed out clearly. In that respect there is a mutual vigilance, and it is if this vigilance is lacking on their part that students will feel obliged to justify the behaviour and attitude of their teacher.

Sometimes the teacher's behaviour may seem contrary to how you feel a teacher should act, but you may not be in any real position to judge. The teacher may appear judgemental, rude, unkind, or deluded but he or she may be fully conscious of how they appear, and be using certain words and mannerisms as a challenge. To know the worth of a teacher, it is necessary to spend as much time as possible with them. Students who rush to judgement based on initial contact or exposure to charismatic utterances may deceive themselves as well as others. Students must learn to act like a water-filter – filtering out any pollution so as to absorb only pure water.

Listening regularly helps train the mind to be focused. We also have to sink our teeth into the practice and not just hold on to the wrapper (the teacher) surrounding even the sweetest-tasting teachings. The best teacher will themselves have been an excellent student.

Though students may support the teacher by looking after their material needs, the kind of generosity that lavishes the teacher with expensive gifts is questionable. The best way of pleasing the teacher is by practising and applying their teachings. Many teachers are not liberated, and have their own issues to work on, yet they can still offer an authentic understanding of the Path to Liberation. They have spent years on the Path and have the right to encourage others to walk it.

It is a student's discernment that will protect them from the curse of the path to awakening, namely self-righteousness or involvement in a cult that becomes the breeding ground for arrogance or manipulation. It is those who make the least effective contribution to awakening who boast the loudest. Unwise teachers often have their own agenda, namely building a spiritual empire, and their students then become pawns to that end.

The genuine teacher has a single priority – to make resources and tools available which enable their students to discover depths of insight, realise the truth of things and live a free life. Out of awareness and love, genuine teachers dedicate their lives to the welfare of others. As teachers, we are first and foremost servants of the Dharma.

# THE PURSUIT OF
# POPULARITY

*In an unawakened life, this process has us in its grip. This particular chain of cause and effect affects us all, from the most powerful institutions or individuals to the weakest members of society.*

When we think of the material world, we think of its size, the sheer enormity and extent of it. We easily overlook the significance of the mental world that makes every perception of the material world possible. Our inner life is also a tremendous powerhouse of activity, but at a more subtle level. There is as much to notice going on within us as there is outside. The mental world works according to the same principle as the material world, in a particular chain of cause and effect identified by Buddhist teachers. In an unawakened life, this process has us in its grip. This particular chain of cause and effect affects us all, from the most powerful institutions or individuals to the weakest members of society. It is essential to look at the way this sequence works in our life and the impact that it has.

1. The process begins with contact.
2. From contact to feeling.
3. From feeling to desire.
4. From desire to attachment.
5. From attachment to becoming.

We make contact with an idea, or an impression, as it comes to one of our senses. It produces a feeling, perhaps a pleasant feeling. From that pleasant feeling arises a desire. That desire can lead us to attachment. From what we have grasped on to, we get caught up in and then the ego feeds on this sequence of feelings, desires, attachments and becoming. We can look at this process in personal, social, political, corporate and global terms. In addition, as long it goes unexamined, it will lead to various forms of suffering for the individual, for humanity and the earth through the unwillingness to examine our desires and what follows as a result.

Every time we feel caught up in this process, we need to stop. We need to see whether we can act from a basis of awareness, love and wisdom, rather than from desire, attachments and becoming. If we can sacrifice one major desire, we can take a great leap forward towards effective, lasting understanding. If we sacrifice the frantic pursuit of pleasure, popularity and profit, we can then focus our attention on wise action. We know then that this sequence has lost its hold over our life.

It is easy to see this chain of causal conditions in far too many politicians, who seem obsessed with becoming respected or having a place in history. Their obsession with popularity causes presidents and prime ministers to become slaves to opinion polls. Every initiative gets measured not by its value, nor by its moral necessity but according to what the data reveals through market research. They never seem to take risks. They only make decisions based on what the market says will give them least hassle.

The democratic process itself colludes in this submission to opinion polls since popularity acts as a prerequisite for politicians to keep their jobs. The need for popularity with the general public inhibits wise and compassionate action due to fear of public disapproval.

When we try to please as many people as possible with the minimum amount of upset, we betray ourselves, our integrity and sense of dignity. We then try to ensure right down to the last micro-detail that our popularity will sustain itself for as long as possible. We then compromise deep values, thus placing self-interest above all other considerations. There is no substitute for wise and compassionate action based on justice, accountability and a skilful assessment of reality.

In the pursuit of popularity, we strive to make an impression on others. We cannot hide the intention behind such striving. More than anything else, we want our name to be known. This shows there is nothing left to reflect any kind of vision. We reduce ourselves to being a crowd-pleaser, to the point where we might even get pleasure from upsetting people, as long as they talk about us. We become slaves to feelings, desires, attachments in order to become somebody important.

We've become conditioned through going from one desire to another or blind pursuit of the same ends. There is no vision when we have succumbed to such striving. As one entertainer wryly commented: 'You can spend your whole life trying to be popular but, at the end of the day, the size of the crowd at your funeral will be largely dictated by the weather.'

# Seeing Through Thoughts

*To study the mind is to know the mind. Meditation makes an important contribution to inner work: stillness is the nest from which we observe thoughts arising and passing.*

The development of awareness comes right at the point where thinking about something begins. For example, when I say that this is a watch, my words are in accordance with the actuality. That is clear and obvious thought. Nevertheless, it can also be the point of departure from reality into reaction, a leap we so often take from the factual to the speculative. We start by saying, 'This is a watch', and then we go on, 'I wonder what the exact time is. Am I late for something? I have so much to do and so little time. How many tasks can I complete before the end of the week?' The simple fact of seeing the watch quickly becomes cluttered with other associations and ideas.

When we find ourselves spinning off into thoughts that are further and further from the reality that generated them, we need to become aware and notice what sparks our indulgent thinking. Our observation may not arrest the stream of concerns immediately, and they may continue to be a nuisance, but through observation we can begin to find the inner intelligence and clear comprehension that doesn't believe in all that compulsive speculation. Through learning to observe in this way, we can save ourselves much confusion in life.

Through observation, we find that the amount of thinking we need to engage in is considerably reduced. Take the 'future'. We can learn to distinguish what part of our thinking about this is realistic planning and what is futile hype or worry. Similarly, when we remember past experiences, we can learn to discard extraneous guilt or pleasure that fills the time but reveals nothing. If we are willing to develop our understanding, we reduce considerably all forms of obsessive thinking. Through such practice, we can find a much greater sense of inner space and contentment.

When we are lost in thinking, we direct our energy towards it. When we observe, however, we stand back quietly, and so transfer our energy back from the circle of thinking into the experience of witnessing it. When we are totally caught up in our thinking, there is nothing much else going on for us. We live in a mind-made world, a thought world, and confuse our ideas with reality; the speculative nature of thought mixes with actual experience. Through observation and non-attachment, thoughts that seemed large, real and consuming begin to recede into the background.

Our minds move in a very small field when trapped in thought. Despite the seemingly endless number of possible ramifications of an issue, our thoughts about it are a limited product of memory, conditioning and experience. We can train ourselves to let go of thinking, to settle into what is, focus our attention and engage in a pure, choiceless awareness. To study the mind is to know the mind. Meditation makes an important contribution to inner work: stillness is the nest from which we observe thoughts arising and passing. The practice of sitting completely still, with our back straight, slows down thinking. We become more meditative as the mind gets less speedy. This inner development eliminates the agitation that goes along with too much thinking. The bare observation of thought leads thought itself into a more balanced relationship to events. When the mind is in touch with the fact of an event, we have cast off compulsive mental behaviour.

As the witness, we see our thoughts appearing and disappearing in an unproblematic way. In such observation, we find a space. In the space before thought arises, there is much to be discovered. Through this awareness, words, concepts and images fade from significance. The true significance of non-conceiving, non-forming, and non-concluding emerges.

As we develop a greater inner space, we come to a silence of being where thoughts fail to have any impact. Thoughts either come to a stop, or lose their power to invade consciousness or impinge upon silence. In that utter silence of being, where thought has no part and no impact, everything is revealed – simply, clearly and immediately.

# INDIVIDUAL
# PSYCHOTHERAPY

*To attend to a few personal problems without examining your
whole relationship to existence blocks the opportunity for an
enlightened life.*

One's heart reaches out to people who experience unresolved inner
problems. The poor often have to live with their personal issues no
matter how much attention they need. They may turn to their
Gods or priests if they are believers, or simply struggle on through
thick and thin with nobody to turn to. It has been said often enough
that psychotherapists are the new priests of the middle classes.
Those with disposable income can see a therapist on a regular basis.
For such people, their relationship with their psychotherapist is
very important. It is the opportunity to unload problems, to try to
reach some understanding of what's going on inside them. A few
people with spiritual and religious commitments also see psychotherapists. They may feel that their spiritual practices or religion and therapy treat different aspects of themselves. Others may
take the view that one-to-one contact on a regular basis with any
wise and caring person, untrained in therapy, who can listen and
respond can provide the same benefits. Others will strongly disagree.

It is questionable whether it is the language and techniques of
psychotherapy, or the capacity to listen and support, that are more
significant. It is possible that if there were wise spiritual teachers,
priests or simply wise individuals available to see individuals on a
regular basis, the benefits would be as great. It seems that people
need someone to explore their issues with. Psychotherapists fulfil
this important function, though it's not easy.

109

In the introduction to *Light on Enlightenment*, I wrote that psychotherapy 'relies mostly on the exchange of language between therapist and client to understand *certain* features of the make-up of the personality. Generally speaking, psychotherapy examines issues of self involved in relationship to matters past, present or future. Psychotherapy explores our attitudes, certain states of mind and the impact of others on our lives . . . I believe neither religion, study nor therapy goes far enough, nor deep enough, into the nature of existence. Many in those respected fields would agree.' Much is offered in the field of psychotherapy, and new forms of psychotherapy emerge every year or two as therapists struggle to find suitable methods for their clients. Much of their work is at the individual level. No matter how many hours of therapy they undergo, individuals will rarely experience anything as profound as the full realisation of the emptiness of the ego and the liberation that emerges from an awakened life. In this respect it is important to realise the Buddhist goal is different.

Not surprisingly, many people find themselves spending years in therapy to help them function adequately in society. With a skilled psychotherapist, clients can learn to handle situations far better, and their old patterns of mind can lose their potency. There is much to be grateful to dedicated psychotherapists for, and they provide an important service for the middle classes. The ability to manage difficult circumstances better acts as a stepping stone to an awakened life.

One important contribution to an awakened life is a deep association with like-minded people. A spiritual community acts as a support and invaluable resource. It is hard to imagine that consciousness can truly awaken, based on two or three sessions of therapy a week. Individual psychotherapy is no substitute for association with a network of wise friends and contacts.

Spiritual community is a great jewel of life, incomparable and worthy of attention. Until psychotherapy incorporates the importance of spiritual community, it will be asking too much of the individual to live wisely and happily with social and family circumstances. The self alone cannot cope with pressures from the past and present, and fears about the future, so some people find themselves involved in weekly therapy as a coping mechanism.

Psychotherapy could include much more than it is willing to at present. This means looking at lifestyle, money, right livelihood, pleasure, possessions, study, religious beliefs and unexamined cultural conditioning. Intensive retreats, a palpable silence, depths of meditation, dying to the self, transcendent and imminent realisations truly transform our lives. That's not easy and it will take the support of like-minded people. We have to be honest with ourselves. Some individuals only want psychotherapy so they can get through each week as skilfully as possible. That's fine, as long as they're clear about their intention. Others will need to look outside psychotherapy to plunge into the liberating depths of existence.

We must not forget that the mind is the governing influence. Mind matters. It does not stand alone but interacts with the rest of life, and with other minds. To attend to a few personal problems without examining your whole relationship to every facet of this breathtaking existence blocks the opportunity for an enlightened life. There is no point in settling for anything less than the best. The best is enlightenment. The highest tribute we can pay to the mind is to enlighten it.

# INNER CHANGE

*Once you discover a sustainable inner motivation, you will find
that tools become available to you to work on mind and body.
You will take steps.*

There was an eccentric Sufi sage who received visitors regularly to
his home. They came with all sorts of questions about issues affecting their lives. One day, some of the visitors arrived to find the sage
seated with a plate of hot peppers in front of him. He was eating one
after the other. The visitors were puzzled and asked the sage why
he was eating so many hot peppers. He replied: 'I am waiting for a
sweet one to come along so I know what it tastes like.'

The harsh truth is that we live far too much of our life repent-
ing errors of judgement. We go on doing the same old things in the
same old way, with the forlorn hope that the time will come when
everything will become much easier. We keep biting on hot peppers, experience all the discomfort that goes with it, and wait for
them to change into something sweet. They won't.

What makes inner change come about? One of the most important factors is neither means nor tools; it is motivation. We need a
firm and sustainable resolve to make important inner changes – acting out issues and talking endlessly about them is not enough. We
may not even be consciously aware of this motivation. For example,
we may have a transforming experience and feel a change within
ourselves that takes us in a fresh direction. We still have to be motivated to follow it through, however.

After the Buddha's enlightenment, he initially lacked the motivation to give teachings and practices to others on an awakened life.
He felt that other people would not understand the significance and
depth of what he had realised. It was a pure-hearted person in the
village of Bodh Gaya who convinced the Buddha that there were

people around 'with little dust in their eyes' who were ready to realise an awakened life. The Buddha then set off to walk for several days to Sarnath to speak with his friends about liberation here and now.

If you want to change, you must cultivate conscious motivation. Once you discover a sustainable inner motivation, you will find that tools become available to you to work on mind and body. You will take steps. You may proceed slowly and with uncertainty, but you will move forward.

A helpful first step to inner change is to describe your mind-state at length – tape-record your description, write it down, tell someone else about it. Try not to reduce the experience to a simple cause-and-effect relationship. Can you see another way of looking at the situation? Changing your attitude will make a real difference. The process of self-inquiry includes quiet reflection, discussion, listening to talks, selective reading and meditation. It is your inner motivation that will give you the determination to do this. We explore to know the nature of the mind, to examine its construction.

It is helpful to look at the mind in impersonal rather than personal terms. To keep believing this state of mind is happening to 'me' and affecting 'me' is part of the problem, not part of the cure. Treat the mind instead as an unfolding process. Unless we give up our obsession with 'me', we will never know inner freedom. We must go deep within to experience the ground of experience. When we find stillness, there is nothing to do and nowhere to go. We have come home. When we are able to renew that experience, even for just a few short moments, we develop a certain inner power, a firm and settled confidence. From that place, we can begin to look at the subtle areas of the mind.

There is stillness in the heart of things. Stillness is not something we can hold, or create, but we can be still. When we experience inner depth and insight, we can nullify many problems. Clarity becomes a conscious, daily experience, and we are truly on the way to enlightenment. A sweetness at the heart of things becomes available to us, and we would not swap it for the world – literally as well as metaphorically.

# PROJECTIONS

*The deeper meaning of darshan is insight or exposure to teachings. The darshan of life is seeing into it, seeing into the nature of existence and thereby being at peace with it.*

The word for seeing in Sanskrit is *darśana*. In popular usage, darshan has come to mean a meeting with a guru. People who are immature in the spiritual field are easily impressed with a guru who stares into their eyes or places his hands on top of their head to direct energy into it. They start to worship another's physical existence and make them a celebrity in their life. They imagine their guru has *siddhis* (paranormal powers) and a powerful charisma. They forget the power of their own projection, and that our mind plays a considerable role in whatever we perceive. Authentic teachers can touch us deeply through their eyes or loving hands, as can other wise and kind people. Our inner life comes first, not the claims we make about the guru.

The deeper meaning of darshan is insight or exposure to teachings. The darshan of life is seeing into it, seeing into the nature of existence and thereby being at peace with it. It is the key to an awakened existence. Imbalance arises in our lives due to the frequency and intensity of our projections, which distort our direct darshan with existence. Strong projections prevent us from distinguishing our mental stuff from anything else: we depart further and further from the reality of the situation. These projections reveal themselves in three primary ways:

1. Desire that gets charged with projections.
2. Conceit, when the 'I' is charged with projections.
3. Opinions that project notions of self-importance or lack of self-worth.

Projections enable us to build ourselves up, put ourselves down, and distort our perception of a situation. If we light a candle in a draught, the flame is blown about and the power of the light is diminished. Similarly, when the mind is blown about, it reveals less, or invests different situations with unnecessary importance. The ego is inseparably involved in projections, and it takes practice to distinguish ego projections from reality. Our projections create a sequence of ideas, often loosely knit together. These then take on their own importance and we begin to believe in them and allow a prejudice to build up that is strengthened through repetition. Soon the mind can only see in one way.

The endless repetition of these projections makes a deep groove within our mind. We keep running along this groove, living out its projections. We begin to believe implicitly in what the mind presents. But once we see projections for what they are, we develop the capacity to focus on bare actuality. A calm mind is a mirror that reflects reality.

There is an old story of a Buddhist monk in Sri Lanka. As he was walking along the road, a very beautiful woman came running towards him. The monk was walking mindfully, quietly appreciating nature and experiencing his feet touching the earth. As the woman ran by, she gave him a big beaming smile. Five minutes later, a young man came running down the same country road and said to the monk, 'Did you see a beautiful woman go this way?' The monk looked up and smiled and said, 'No, I just saw a set of teeth go by!' Much loved by monks, this story has been passed on in monasteries for generations. It sounds austere in a conventional sense, but it's a way of getting a point over about connection with bare actuality.

We live a noble way of life when we cut through superfluous states of mind to experience extraordinary delight in the miracle of existence. We encounter wonderful, humane and caring people, appreciating them whilst feeling no excitement about their arrival or sorrow at their departure. Living wisely ends the tendency to proliferate ideas about what we perceive. There is a wisdom and joy to this way of being in the world.

# MIRACLES

*What is the point of being woken up from the dead if we are
only going to go back to the same old selfish ways?*

There is a world-famous guru in South India, widely known for
making miracles. His devotees claim he can produce something out
of nothing – sacred ash, gold rings and Seiko watches. People arrive
by the jumbo jet-load to see him, hoping he will perform miracles,
or at least glance towards them. One of his devotees told me of the
guru's 'incredible powers'. She said that when he produced sacred
ash at his ashram, he simultaneously made it come out of the eyes,
ears, nose and mouth of photographs of himself hanging in the
homes of devotees around the world. She asked me what I thought
of such powers. I told her I thought it was fiction. She insisted it
was true. I gave her all the details of how she could get in touch with
me, and said I would fly immediately anywhere to witness such a
miracle in a devotee's home. I said if it is true then his power defies
all my understanding about the nature of things. Something cannot
come from nothing. If it is anything more than sleight of hand, I
added, I will be on the next train to South India, and I promise I
will prostrate to the guru for the rest of my life. I am still waiting to
hear from her.

A few months later a friend visited another Indian guru, who
handed her a video secretly circulating around ashrams in India. It
showed a film of the South Indian guru performing his 'miracles'.
Slowing down the film, to a frame at a time, the friend said she
could clearly see the sleight of hand. The guru could not perform
miracles after all – only party tricks.

However, there is much that we cannot explain. One of the
important areas of wondrous miracles is healing. There are people
who have this power. They engage in contact with other people

116

that affects their energy. We cannot explain it, but people get well. We need to take such 'miraculous' healing seriously. Something remarkable can take place in an atmosphere of love, direct contact and care that shifts things within. We should not dismiss such healings quickly, but keep our hearts open to what loving people can offer each other.

Religion often has an infatuation with magical powers, including

- Passing through walls.
- Walking on water.
- Flying through the air.
- Reaching out to touch the sun and moon.
- Waking up the dead.
- Bringing people back to life.
- Remembering countless past lives.
- Disappearing and reappearing.
- Making something out of nothing.
- Appearing in different places at the same time.

These miracles and others become proof in the minds of devotees of their leader's miraculous powers over the forces of nature. There is a belief that these miracles offer some kind of proof of attainment. Despite the massive amount of attention given to such beliefs, I cannot find anyone who has such powers to defy the laws of nature.

What is the point of being woken up from the dead if we are only going to go back to the same old selfish ways? What is the point of walking on water if we are only going to become arrogant on land? Miracles have to be understood in a different way. For the liberated ones, the entire list of miracles certainly has meaning. They have woken up from the dead, come back to life and then recall the countless rebirths of their ego in the past. They know they are no longer prisoners of the elemental forces. Land, water and air hold no grip over their consciousness. Awakened Ones have realised they are nothing and out of it has come everything. For most people, however, there is the cycle of birth and death, like endlessly appearing, disappearing and reappearing waves in the great ocean of existence.

117

The liberated ones effortlessly encompass the entire movement of existence from what is in their hand to the furthest sun and moon in other galaxies. It is this discovery of unexcelled liberation which ranks as the true miracle: the world of birth and death loses its grip. Something miraculous has happened to a consciousness that has shaken itself free from its conventional moorings to embrace the birthless and the deathless.

There is nothing to be gained from this world, and there is nothing the world can take away. Some liberated ones from various traditions share their awakening, enabling others to see, hear and walk again.

# THE PRACTICE OF UNDERSTANDING

# WHAT MATTERS?

*When we are caught up in superficiality, it really matters to us if
our clothes don't fit very well, if the car isn't running smoothly,
if the weather is grey, or if our team loses.*

We look at life with religious, scientific, philosophical or artistic
eyes. Or even with the eyes of indifference. Those ways of looking
at life – although legitimate – come from a particular perspective.
As we move through life, we notice the frequency our attention
alights upon things. Our life is propelled along from one thing to
another, and we come to think this is the only way to be. We rarely
find time to stop and see something small and incidental. How do
we experience a single flower? Are we willing to experience the
cloud moving through the sky? How do we experience moving our
arms to pick something up?

For some, religion has traditionally offered a prop to an inse-
cure consciousness. Some people take up a religion because it offers
the promise of safety after death. Individuals are often unable to
come to terms with death, and owing to the uncertainty of existence, the assurance of an eternal heaven has immense appeal. Such
a belief may bring the mind to a state of quiet, of feeling saved and
secure. However, this self-assurance does not mean to say we are
coming closer to Truth, or God.

Is it possible to live with a different awareness, without reaching out to believe in anything? A man said to the Buddha that if he
was to explore Dharma he first had to have the answers to certain
questions. He refused to engage in meditation until he got the
answers that he wanted. 'I want to know, how did this world begin?
How is it going to end? I must know whether or not I will exist after
death.'

The Buddha asked, 'Did I say I would give you these answers?

Did I ever promise to tell you the answers to these questions?' These questions are not the concern of the Dharma, only of religious and scientific speculators. Being preoccupied with metaphysical speculations is not conducive to awareness, depth, penetration, non-attachment, or the discovery of the true nature of things. Is it possible for us to let go of these endless futile speculations about the beginning and end of the world, and life after death? Is it going to make any difference whether we agree or disagree with the possibility of life after death?

If we let go of such speculation, we find space instead to observe the realities of our daily existence. We see and observe the way our senses are pushed and pulled. When we are caught up in superficiality, it really matters to us if our clothes don't fit very well, if the car isn't running smoothly, if the weather is grey or if our team loses. To live wisely and adventurously enables us to experience far more excellent things in life than these.

Excellence is joy, insight into things, stillness of mind, love, wisdom, and peace. Genuine awareness rejects a narrow vision of life for a vision that explores spaciousness, takes risks, and is marked with excellence. Everything is examined, and only what is superfluous to excellence is rejected, especially the obsessive struggling, striving and pushing onwards into involvement with things we know really don't matter. In a wise life, our awareness of what matters embraces four areas – the world around us; our body; the state of our heart; and the state of our mind. We neither shirk nor avoid what takes place in our environment: we are aware of our impact on it. We examine the way we use our physical life, including what we put into our body, and how we treat it. We cultivate our heart through clear expressions of love, generosity and joy. We are aware of our thoughts, and know what influences our intentions and attitudes, and what kind of concepts and impressions we have absorbed. If we attend to all four areas, we won't neglect anything that matters, and we will begin to see the interrelatedness of all things.

There is something that we might call 'spiritual' about this kind of awareness. It has the potential for remarkable revelations that will end all our speculation about the metaphysical issues. There is an indescribable joy for those who go deeper than the conceptual layers of the mind.

# LOVE AND ATTACHMENT

*'Nothing whatsoever is worth being attached to.'*

One of my four teachers, Venerable Ajahn Buddhadasa, perhaps the foremost Buddhist teacher of the twentieth century, applied the teachings to everyday life rather than just monastic life. He was ordained at the age of twenty and spent sixty-seven years living in a forest in southern Thailand and teaching about the importance of Dharma in daily life. He once told me that he based all his Dharma teachings on a comment of the Buddha, '*Sabbe Dhamma nalam abhinivesaya*'. In the Pali language of the original text, *sabbe* means 'all'; *dhamma* means 'the teachings and everything in the physical, emotional, mental and spiritual worlds', and *nalam abhinivesaya* means 'not worth being identified with'. Taken together, the four words translate as 'Nothing whatsoever is worth being attached to'.

In the very first conversation I had with Ajahn Buddhadasa, I asked him a question about life though I cannot remember the nature of the question. At the time, I was a twenty-five-year-old traveller living out of a backpack. In response, he looked at me and pulled his saffron robe off his shoulder with a flamboyant gesture. He held it in his raised hand and said, 'If you really want to understand the nature of existence, then nothing whatsoever is worth being attached to or identified with. In my case, that includes being a monk and having a robe.' Then he called over a novice and told him to take me to a hut in the forest to reflect on the importance of non-attachment.

Ajahn Buddhadasa's teachings were diverse but their essence was succinct. Being identified with possessions, people and ideas is seen as a positive value in our society. We cannot imagine living without identifying with our country, family, work – and certainly with ourselves. We cannot imagine an existence in which we are not attached to our values, aims and directions, or to the people we know and love. We believe it is essential to be attached to certain aspects of life, and that without such attachments, we would be cold, detached and alienated from life itself.

Non-attachment seems to go against reason; it seems to go against being human. We have to look deeper to fully understand the significance of non-attachment, especially in view of the positive value that Western psychologists place on attachment. Buddhism teaches that attachments bedevil the mind. Rather than divide attachments into positive (such as family) and negative (smoking, selfish pursuits), Buddhists believe that any attachment reveals a blind spot, an inability to stay directly in touch with the way things are, rather than how we would like them to be.

For example, we often confuse attachment with love. Attachment is in fact like a virus that eats up love, although we may not realise it.

When we love someone, we genuinely care for him or her. We give our time, energy, and attention to them. When circumstances cause that person to step out of our life, we might react with resentment, despair or jealousy. We suffer over our loss. We may even offer that as proof of our love, our logic being, 'If I didn't love this person, I wouldn't be suffering.'

In Dharma language, suffering is the result of attachment, not love. Such attachment arises due to the desire to hold on to the vested interests of the self. The teachings point to our capacity to be free from all 'grief, sorrow, lamentation and despair'. A true statement of love shows itself in the depth of our connection and the wisdom that acknowledges change, for better or worse. We have the capacity to love others with all our heart but we do not possess them. We have to be very clear about that. We practise in daily life to keep our hearts open, to love others and to be present for others in time of need. If we look into our heart, we can distinguish between what is love and what happens when we treat loved ones as a possession. To know and understand the difference between the two is a sign of wisdom.

To explore the difference between love and attachment ends despair. Others have the right to move out of our lives. If they care for us, they will not have wished to inflict suffering upon us. If we love them, we will not experience despair when such changes take place in our life. Our love will stay constant without sliding into unhappiness through attachment to wanting things on our own terms. This selfless love truly expresses an enlightened understanding.

# THE SUBSTANCE
# VIEW

*As something catches our attention, our feelings and
thoughts define it and give it substance.*

When we look carefully at our experience of the world, we see that
it is made up of a panorama of events. These include situations,
experiences, sensations, thoughts and perceptions too numerous
for us ever to be able to count or record them all. Life is a seemingly
endless sequence of events. If we look back over our life, there are
only a limited number of these events that have made an impression, that matter to us. We have selected certain events from this
vast symphony of personal history, invested them with substance,
and made them into something.

How do we go about isolating a few things out of the bombard-
ment of experience and solidifying them? As something catches our
attention, our feelings and thoughts define it and give it substance.
Such habits start as cobwebs and end up as cables. I call this 'the
substance view'. Coming out of the substance view puts us in touch
with the ongoing process of life. I am reminded of the Buddha's
teaching on seeing process rather than 'selfness'. When we
experience directly, in seeing there is just seeing; in hearing, just
hearing; in smelling, tasting and touching, just smelling, tasting
and touching; in remembering, just remembering; in feelings and
thinking; just feelings and thinking; in knowing, just knowing.
There is something enlightening about this understanding, since
we feel neither trapped nor stuck with anything. We give substance
neither to life nor death. We experience feelings and emotions as
expressions that arise and pass.

When we forget to attend to the arising and passing of

thoughts, we pay a price, since the self gives substance to something that inherently lacks substance. Our lives totally belong to this vast unfolding process. To imagine that anyone has ever been substantial, or become substantial, is a gross self-deception.

We define ourselves through what we think about. Thought determines the way our lives appear to us. Our knowledge of ourselves and our actions in the world come from what we think about. There is also something uncanny about thoughts. The moment we deliberately place our attention on a stream of thoughts, they disappear out of the field of awareness. For example, you are thinking about what you will say when you have an interview for a new job. There are some fears and anxieties influencing your thinking. The moment you decide to look directly at your thoughts, however, they stop arising in your mind at that very moment.

Because thoughts give substance and weight to all matters, we never want to neglect the fact that thoughts are only thoughts. They are not necessarily a true reflection of the bare facts of a situation. For thoughts to accurately mirror facts, our mind needs to be remarkably clear and our heart warm and steady. Our attention needs to be underpinned with wisdom; anything else will distort our perceptions and subsequent thoughts. Submitting to one foolish stream of thoughts or words invites more of the same.

Investing more and more thoughts in a situation builds up the substance view of it, potentially to the point where the issue overwhelms us. Once we view life through this filter of 'my' thoughts about certain events, people, and experiences, we have entered a personal worldview masquerading as true reality. We can give a substance view to anything from the past, present or future. We can project thoughts on to life and death, thus giving them a substantial significance. We are afraid to die since death is the cessation of the view that our 'self' is substantial. In reality, nothing has any inherent substance. That includes our 'self'. There is no soul, nothing permanent. Investment and projections are what make things difficult.

In this vast, unfolding symphony of existence, we are constantly selecting things, fixing them, believing in them, and basing our lives on them – and we are afraid to question this. We think that we know who we are by what has happened to us in the past. We feel the need to have a clear idea of the future. We believe that without the substance view there won't be anything to hang on to, and we will be utterly confused and lost. Can we challenge that view? We need to if we wish to live an enlightened life.

# THE PROLIFERATION
# OF THOUGHTS

*If we cannot stop the relentless march of thoughts, we will be
overwhelmed with thinking. The wise choice to practise 'not
thinking about' is ignored.*

Thoughts can go on and on: it seems impossible to exhaust their
determination to perpetuate themselves. The proliferation of
thoughts around a particular issue determines our perception of it.
It is as if situations have a compelling magnetism and our mind gets
addicted to them. Our habits of thinking tend to be automatic, and
often go on relentlessly. For example, some people constantly
analyse: everything has to be broken down into bits and pieces.
Other people are stuck in logic: everything must fit into their own
system of thinking, otherwise it can't be any good. We are easily
caught in our own models and systems of thought – like fish in a
net.

There is a place for analysis and subtle inquiry into subtlety;
and for skilful discrimination and investigation. But thought easily
becomes repetitive and involved in areas where it is not appropriate, applicable or liberating. We know this from our own
experience; our inner wisdom will frequently tell us that something
is simply not worth thinking about. If we cannot stop the relentless
march of thoughts, we will be overwhelmed with thinking. The
wise choice to practise 'not thinking about' is ignored.

What is it that makes us hold on to our thoughts and cherish
them so much that we carry them around like sacks of potatoes on
our back? Are we using thought for security? They may make us
feel we know about reality, and that seems reassuring. Are we using
thought to help us feel okay, to help us feel that we know? Are we

using thought to create problems and conflicts? Are we afraid to let go of our ideas about reality?

It would be absurd to try to stop thought, to destroy it completely or drop our intellect. Rather, we have to reduce our dependency on our thoughts and our accumulated knowledge as ways of understanding events. To truly acknowledge the severe limitations of thought signals the beginning of awakening. The more we build up the importance of a thing, the more we separate it from the symphony of life. What are we holding on to philosophically, spiritually, emotionally, conceptually, religiously or politically? For our thoughts play an extraordinary part in all those areas, whether born from interpretation of experience, beliefs, or viewpoints.

We can boil our practice down to a simple, regular exercise: reminding ourselves that the streams of thoughts are fleeting, transitory and merely interpretations of events, not statements of true reality. If we allow this truth to run deep within us, it will help us moderate our reliance on our concepts and views of the way things are. If we can understand the place and limitations of the field of thought, liberation and freedom are not something down the road, but already immediately accessible. We will be able to see space between our thoughts, and it will seem ridiculous to identify with their flow. It will seem immature to give prominence to a set of thoughts because we will know and realise that a thought is just a thought – no more and no less.

Let us not make much of persistent thoughts nor feed them. Let us be free from the tyranny of identification with thoughts. Let us be liberated from all manifestations of psychological imprisonment.

# WHAT SELF?

*We think about me, me, me. This is not unusual, but it is*
*certainly a miserable condition to be in.*

The concept of no-self in the Buddhist tradition is paradoxical and
nearly impossible to comprehend. On the face of it, if there's no
self, we don't exist – so, what's the point? It's difficult to get a feeling for this concept, as the one thing we seem to take for granted is
our 'self'. When Buddhists come along and question the obvious, it
seems to insult our intelligence. We can either dismiss their view
altogether or we can explore whether there is any value in it. Do I
have a true reality? Am I substantial? Is there simply a process
unfolding without any essence called self to it? This question concerned the Buddha, so perhaps it ought to concern us as well.

A useful way to approach this area of 'self' and 'no-self' is to
start with what is familiar in our conventional way of seeing, and
then explore whether we can see in a different way. When we look
at what constitutes our personal 'self', we see a body, feelings, perceptions, views, and mental formations that consciousness holds
together. When we speak of being a human being, we're referring
to a dynamic, living process that was born in time, exists in time
and will pass in time. This is who we are, and we can't speak of ourselves outside this body–mind–feeling stream of activity.

We see how the degree of our identification with this process
varies with our experiences. One moment we identify with our
body, another moment with our state of mind. We become
involved with one feature of our self and then another. We make
claim to all of them. This reinforces our sense of self. We think
about me, me, me. This is not unusual, but it is certainly a miserable condition to be in.

At other times, the power of our belief in self seems

131

questionable. This can occur spontaneously as we meditate – our personal history and self-structure then seem less relevant, and the influence of the past fades. This allows us to stay in touch with the here and now, so that intimations of other ways of seeing can emerge. There is bare experience of the impressions from sights and sounds; ideas or memories show themselves and pass. It becomes clear that there is no solid self. Very, very clear. There is nothing to this 'I' unless it's caught up in the unfolding process called body and mind.

Some psychologists believe that we have to build up a sense of self before we can be ready to understand the absence of a substantial self. They believe that those who can't accept themselves, who put themselves down, have a low sense of self-worth. So it has to be built up, they claim. This is a misunderstanding – to put it politely. The real problem with people who keep attacking themselves, putting themselves down and feeling worthless is that they cling to a strong sense of self.

Their problem comes from having placed layers and layers of negativity on to the self: they retain a strong sense of 'I, me and mine' due to these negative influences. Those who hold on to an inflated sense of self and those who have a deflated sense of self share the same problem: a daily preoccupation with 'I, me and mine'. To see through all of that simultaneously dissolves the warped notion of a solid self. That's what the Buddha keeps pointing at. It also puts an end to that miserable way of being in the world.

The constructed self lacks real presence. There is nothing whatsoever concrete about it. Once we become aware of the insubstantial nature of self, any preoccupation with the two extremes of the inner life – those who put themselves up and those who put themselves down – is dissolved.

As we move from gross to subtle observation in our meditation, meditation experience becomes more refined. All the layers imposed upon self fall away as a result of insight, reflection and clear seeing. We forget all that we project on to ourselves through self-importance or self-rejection.

Reflecting seriously on these matters dissolves the anguish, hurt and frustration that characterise preoccupation with self. The 'I' has the same significance as a line drawn on water. A self-existence that is separate from everything else belongs to a fictionalised view of the world. The appearance of self only exists in conjunction with everything, never by itself. There is no independent self-existence. Belief in boosting up and putting down the self belongs to the realm of virtual reality.

Through insight, the obsessive self loses its significance, meaning and relevance. When the teachings speak of the importance of realising the emptiness of self, we now naturally recognise what that means. To be truly free ends the inflated and deflated ego. There is an ungraspable freedom that not even this 'I' can claim belongs to it. Then we are grounded in the nature of things. This is unsurpassable.

# THE EGO

*CEOs and directors desperately want to be thought well of. They hate having their motives examined or being the butt of jokes.*

There is a commonly held view that spiritual people have suspended permanently their critical faculties. We are expected to be gentle, peaceful and never in any circumstances express distaste for what we disapprove of. If we do criticise any sections of society, it reads as if we are making a blanket condemnation of everybody in that section of society. For example, there are CEOs (Chief Executive Officers) and directors who perform a wonderful public service. They have not become 'fat cats' by awarding themselves substantial incomes or by placing excessive pressures on workers or the environment to maximise profits. That, obviously, is not always the case. I believe it is the responsibility of people devoted to the spiritual life to challenge greed and exploitation among the rich and powerful. I read a report in *The Economist*, a weekly British magazine widely read by businessmen, which said, 'plenty of mergers begin with executive boredom'. This is an admission that the condition of our inner life reflects and informs many decisions. It is well known, or if not it ought to be, that those at the top in the corporate world have the least stress. They earn large salaries for relatively little work. Many have the time to be on the board of several companies. Absence of stress seems to leave certain CEOs and their directors wondering what to do to bring more excitement into their comfortable routines. As far as their careers are concerned, they have no further to go: they already occupy the best rooms in the building, and their staff treat them with deference. But they want to continue to make a big impression. *The Economist* reported that the CEO might only have about five years in his position: 'The surest way to make a mark in so short a time is to buy something big.'

A proposal for a massive takeover or a merger will get the attention of the media, investment bankers, shareholders and brokers. The CEO's name becomes better known, thus satisfying his vanity, and the board of directors feel important. For such a CEO, perhaps the letters also stand for 'Chief Ego Officer': *The Economist* refers to 'flagrantly egotistical deals' which ignore the wishes of thousands of staff worldwide whose jobs are put at risk. The economies of 'downsizing' or 'streamlining' are business-speak for throwing numerous workers and middle management on to the scrap heap, making life for them and their families extremely difficult.

The public relations and press officers prepare their publicity releases. Often, unwittingly, they act as a front for the vain ambitions of their employers. CEOs and directors want to be remembered as the architects of a great takeover or merger. They also desperately want to be thought well of. They hate having their motives examined or being the butt of jokes. Their ego is their Achilles heel, and their outer power and wealth often cloak inner poverty. The press and public should lean on their egos more.

We seem to be reluctant to examine business dealings in terms of the states of mind that generate the climate for such egotistical business activity. We remain much more comfortable with examining business in impersonal terms, such as the money involved, the impact of the transaction and the costs of such takeovers. We only look at half the picture, and forget to look at the mind: the state of mind of the people involved can never be separated from the event.

It seems to be of no concern to the public whether the board of directors expresses wisdom, love, compassion or generosity of spirit. Yet these things matter, and they certainly ought to matter more among people of power and influence. We know that many of these people work their way to the top, not out of any deep love and wish to serve others, but as a means to gain power, prestige and profit. We accept this unquestioningly. We expect little from such people and so we get little from them. In our silence, we conform to their egos. It doesn't have to be that way. The ego is vulnerable: it hates being under attack and out of control. It hates losing, and not getting its own way.

We know that far too many people in public life share much in common with the typical CEO. They like to have their own egos massaged, and they will massage each other's egos when it suits them. The modern universities seem to be poor environments to develop authentic understanding of what matters. They have developed into institutions for the acquisition of knowledge; ego-making factories: knowledge is no substitute for wisdom and compassion. Our future leaders need to learn about themselves through inner work. It would be far more productive for society if they spent three years looking deep within and gave a similar time to serving directly those who suffer. Spending three years getting a degree is a poor substitute. Things will only change when we campaign to expect more from people of influence – more kindness, more compassion and understanding. The Goliaths of this world look formidable in the dream world of success and failure. Perhaps the force of public concern will bring them to their knees.

As long as powerful figures live several notches above others in terms of lifestyle, we cannot expect them to have any clue about the hardships that most people pass through daily. Some leaders boast that they began in poverty and worked their way up. A pity. It seems their memories are distressingly short.

Stress reduction courses in the office are not the answer to this global issue. Ego reduction courses would be a lot more productive. Society has little notion of the impact of the ego in public and private life. Nor does it have the resources or tools to work on the ego. If anything, we are impressed with people with big egos. We think that is the way we achieve something. A big ego does achieve something. An even bigger ego!

# The Way of
# Non-attachment

*We must not be afraid to ask ourselves uncomfortable questions.*
*We need to take serious note of our inner responses, and be extra*
*vigilant in these areas.*

I want to look again at non-attachment, since it is such a significant theme in Buddhism. It is a core practice: there is no support for attachment in the teachings. Non-attachment is not the same as detachment, however, which can trigger alienation and indifference. We tend to feel uncomfortable with someone who seems very detached. We suspect that they are cut off from some important feelings. Detachment can communicate a certain coolness, even coldness: it marks a certain withdrawal, while non-attachment shows a non-possessive, non-clinging relationship to matters that arise.

When we are not attached to results, our response can be warm and firm, and we are able to handle the most distressing situations with wisdom. The dissolution of attachment has an extraordinary influence on our emotional life. It releases warmth, kindness, and a profound interconnection that we can feel now that we are no longer caught up in events.

It is useful to investigate our attachments. What am I most attached to? What would generate the most anguish or suffering for me? We must not be afraid to ask ourselves uncomfortable questions. Forethought is easy. Regret is hard. We need to take serious note of our inner responses, and be extra vigilant in these areas. There is nothing and nobody that we can take for granted.

We may need to ask ourselves what we need to develop in ourselves to reduce, or end, an attachment without walking away from the issue. As we go through this process, we may find ourselves renouncing the attachment and its object. However, you can let go of what you are attached to skilfully or unskilfully.

There are stories of people with great wealth who renounce everything as a courageous step towards awakening. Siddhartha Gautama, who became the Buddha, did it 2,500 years ago, for example. Ever since, he has been criticised for fleeing from his wife, Yashodhara, and his week-old son, Rahula, to embark on his quest for enlightenment. It is important to remember that he was a man in crisis. He fled the palace unenlightened, confused and full of self-doubt. Years later, he said it was so painful for him that he could not bear to take a final look at the face of his son in case he changed his mind. Instead, he fled stealthily in the middle of the night, driven by his desire to get to the root of things.

Getting rid of the object of your attachment, however, does not necessarily indicate that your attachment has gone with it. Someone can have very few possessions – just a backpack or a begging bowl – but still be attached to them. It is not how much we have, but the type of relationship we have with existence that determines attachment. Everyone needs to reflect on attachment, whether they live extravagantly or modestly.

Rather than walk out of a comfortable lifestyle, some people stay in the same home and use the same items, but renounce all desire for more – luxuries, expensive goods, greater profits or fancy modernisation of their home. They place all such superficiality behind them. They have more important things to pay attention to. They are utterly non-attached to materialism.

Sometimes the teachings of non-attachment are disconcerting, to put it mildly. They are meant to be.

# MEDITATIVE
# READING

*Drilling the importance of study, study, study into anyone's head
is an act of disservice, sometimes bordering on mental abuse.*

As a result of our education, we may have developed an insatiable
appetite for learning. We have made 'experts' the secular form of
high priests. If they appear on television, they have truly made it:
they are there at the altar of success. Most of us feel rather stupid
in comparison, and sometimes wish we could cram more knowledge into ourselves. But we can never fill this hole. The mind can
only absorb so much knowledge before it starts reacting against
overload.

In their search for satisfaction, some people have transferred
that hunger for intellectual knowledge from the secular to the
spiritual domain. In response, a tremendous number of spiritual
books have become available. Although these books may shed light
on spiritual matters, the true purpose of a spiritual book must be to
make a real difference to its readers' lives, and set them on the road
to enlightenment. Unfortunately, readers may forget that worthwhile spiritual books point to a movement beyond intellectual
satisfaction to a transformed and awakened life.

I have a friend, a university professor who also engaged in
Buddhist practice. He kept a large library at home and possessed
extensive knowledge in spiritual matters as well as in his academic
field. During a meditation retreat, his Buddhist teacher told him to
take a sabbatical and give up reading for a year. The professor said
he had spent so much of his life reading and studying books that at
first it felt unthinkable for him to stop. However, he did. He stopped
reading entirely. He cancelled his magazine subscriptions, avoided

bookshops and even stopped reading the ads on billboards as much as possible. He said that sometimes the impulse to read was so strong that he would go into a public toilet and be fascinated with the graffiti on the walls. He renounced all reading for a full year. When he came back to reading, he said he could see its place in the scheme of things. Non-reading had given him an education, too.

One of the reasons we don't change or come to a deeper understanding despite all our reading is that we don't allow things to run deep inside our being. We are too speedy. We are too greedy for knowledge. We tie ourselves into conceptual models which inhibit the opportunity for deep insights. We should all take a serious look at what we read and how we read. We need to be aware of the ways we relentlessly pump more and more words and information into our heads.

As teachers, students and thoughtful people, we ought to be aware of the message we give to others about the importance of learning. Drilling the importance of study, study, study into anyone's head is an act of disservice sometimes bordering on mental abuse. It generates pressures and stress that have personal, interpersonal and social consequences.

Reading can be a meditation when we make the choice to read more slowly. When something touches us as we read a book, we can stop and allow that response to be absorbed within. We do not have to race on to the next theme to sate the mind's lust for information. Rather than trying to gulp down as much information as possible, take things slowly, meditatively. Reading then becomes a quiet contemplation rather than an obsessive activity.

We can stop at a particular sentence or word and look at it. How does it relate to our experience? We can even close the book and sit with it for a while. It takes time for concepts to register deeply, to reach the heart and stay there. With this approach, reading becomes more selective, focused and meditative. Such reading has the capacity to transform us. Years ago, abbots in Buddhist monasteries gave monks a handful of verses to meditate on for months and months until their understanding flowered.

Reading every paragraph in this book, for instance, may not be a skilful approach. You might only need to contemplate one paragraph very slowly and mindfully over a period for it to awaken your mind, and make a real difference to the quality of your life.

# LEAVES ON A TREE

*We know that every cock can crow on his own dunghill. We are
not even afforded that privilege since the self cannot act as lord
over the condition of the mind.*

Many of the thoughts that arise in our mind are of little consequence. We can compare them to leaves on a tree. When you and I
look up at the tree, we don't say, 'There are too many leaves on that
tree. There should be fewer.' Or, 'Why aren't the leaves falling in
orderly piles?' Blowing around in our mind, our thoughts are like
leaves. Just as it is natural for a tree to produce leaves, so it is
natural for the mind to produce thoughts, but few of them are significant.

Our most important concern is our state of mind. The second
most important concern is our thoughts about our state of mind.
Whatever state of mind arises comes about through various inner
conditions, and it dissolves when these conditions dissolve.
Whatever arises inwardly, passes. This is common, everyday
knowledge, but it tends to be intellectual knowledge. We need to
practise watching our mind-states come and go. There is no substitute for practising the art of watching the arising and passing of
thoughts and ideas.

Thoughts affect our state of mind. Our state of mind can over-
whelm us if we hold on to the way we feel and think about things.
Such thoughts have something destructive about them. They act
like an incendiary device on highly inflammatory material. We have
this illogical idea which says, 'If I keep thinking about this long
enough, I'll come up with an answer,' but what we often come up
with is merely an intensification of our state of mind. We then find
that our mind causes problems to our sense of self. We know that
every cock can crow on his own dunghill. We are not even afforded

141

that privilege since the self cannot act as lord over the condition of the mind.

If we keep thinking long enough, we keep producing more thoughts. We keep pissing against the wind. We then live in a world of remorseless thoughts, under pressure to work things out to our satisfaction. We forget that our endless thinking is a product of our state of mind, not a detached inquiry into the matter at hand. At such times, we need to remember to breathe in and out long and deep, to dance, walk fast, or experience nature so we don't fall prey to our way of thinking.

Experiences rise and fall. States of mind rise and fall. Thoughts rise and fall. Just in a single day, how many states of mind have you and I witnessed? How many different feelings, moods, thoughts and judgements have we seen come and go in ourselves today? One television advertisement for a French car claimed that we have on average 12,000 thoughts a day. God knows how they came to that figure.

We latch on to our thoughts, becoming lost in schemes. The way we think about situations governs our personality and our lives. We forget that our thoughts are only mental formations coming into and passing out of consciousness. They are not statements of true reality. We have the capacity to listen to the deepest place within us before the arising of our thoughts. This allows us to respond in fresh and insightful ways to difficult situations. Wisdom often says, 'This problem isn't worth reacting to.' For example, if we write an angry letter, fax or e-mail, we should sleep on it before deciding whether to send it. Who benefits from an abusive letter? The following day we might change the tone of the letter while still communicating what concerns us.

The Eastern tradition says, '*Atma vidya, atma vidya*' – 'Know thyself, know thyself'. Arriving at the knowledge of how the self is involved in mind-body is a lifelong process.

# RELIGIOUS FORMS

*It we go deeper than the ritual, we can feel a sense of the unknown.*

There is nothing like holding to religious forms – repeating the same thing over and over again – to kill the spirit. We then find the self trapped, thus sacrificing the opportunity to enliven existence. Repeating the same old forms of the tradition, lineage or technique, rather than awakening us, has a numbing effect on the mind.

Instead, we can investigate ways in which we can extend ourselves appropriately. Religious services, rituals and ceremonies have the potential to stimulate the sense of a palpable presence of the Immeasurable amidst the measurable. That may not happen by doing the same old religious routine week after week. We need to remain vigilant around rituals since they have the capacity to numb the mind in the course of time. This means that forms and methodology matter less than the expansion of the heart's awareness and receptivity.

By giving our full care and attention to religious services, we can experience the usefulness and the limitations of ritualistic activities. Form is not something to hold on to. As you deepen your understanding, you can intimately know the place and limitations of your forms of worship. You know what it means to be at peace with rites and rituals and neither live in conflict with rituals nor submit to them: there is a way of being in this world that is free from all that.

It can often feel that stepping back from religious rituals alienates us from them rather than allows us to find a clear view of their significance. Regular participation in rituals builds up a sense of 'who I am'. We forget that as we step back, we also make a step towards something else.

143

Applying this principle inwardly, when we are closely identified with our state of mind our world focuses around our religious beliefs. If you hold the palm of your hand close to your face, all you can see is your hand. Even closer, and you cannot even see that clearly, and you are in darkness. Stepping back allows you to see your hand more clearly. If you distance yourself even further from the hand, you will see even more.

We often have a bias in a particular area. We can cling to worship and rituals or hold to a very dismissive attitude to such forms and practices. Both mind-states resist the opportunity to look at things afresh. Our mind is made up so we do not want to confuse ourselves by questioning our conclusions. Before we can make real changes in our views, we may have to decide whether we really want to change. We may prefer to stay stuck.

If we go deeper than the ritual, we can feel a sense of the unknown. Through meditative awareness, we have the opportunity to be receptive to what is profound, beyond religious forms and language. We can love the formless and our participation in it. We have the capacity to accommodate religious forms without clinging to them. In freedom, and the heart's awakening, the presence or absence of religion in our lives becomes a secondary consideration. For this, we are eternally grateful.

Letting go of the familiar opens the doors of perception. In a steady awareness, much more is made available – interest, sincerity, willingness to learn, joy and appreciation of what we are doing. We appreciate what is happening and the benefits of knowing ourselves well. We have a balanced view of a religious life free from any exaggeration of its importance. So it is not a substitute for wisdom, liberation and enlightenment.

In a deep, expanded sense of well-being, our mind looks after itself. We practise to understand the way of the mind in order to forget the mind and its conditioning. To forget the mind is to forget ourselves. For the ordinary mind to forget itself leads to anguish, but for the mind of deep understanding to forget itself, it leads to remarkable insights into an enlightened life. Involvement in rituals, worship and methodology act as a small branch in the tree of existence. What matters is getting to the root of things.

# ONENESS

*Whether we feel Oneness in the midst of activity or in the quietness of the night, there is something more than just the experience itself. The appreciation of its place in the scheme of things is important, too.*

A schoolteacher was feeling stressed due to the demands of the teenagers in his comprehensive school and the pressure he felt to succeed as a teacher. He decided that he had to get away for the weekend. He drove to Snowdonia in Wales and went hiking in the hills. He climbed one of the higher peaks, sat down and looked all around him. It was breathtaking. He could see the beauty of the countryside, dotted with small villages, and light clouds floating by above them. He suddenly felt this wonderful experience of Oneness. All the problems at the school and in the rest of his personal life faded away. He sat there glowing, enjoying from one moment to the next the sweetness of this totally unexpected experience. It was the first time he had experienced something outside his conventional reality. Many things began to make sense. He stayed up in the hills for the rest of the day. By the end of it, he felt refreshed and ready to go back to the classroom. It was from that time that he began taking a tremendous interest in the field of mystical experience. He regarded that period at the top of the hill as a real turning point in his life.

We often fail to realise the great benefits of experiences such as this, which can help to put so much else into perspective. Sometimes they come knocking on the door of our inner life, but we fail to let them in. This often happens during the night: instead of experiencing the Oneness of all things in the silence, we want to get back to sleep. In the late hours, all may be quiet, extraordinarily quiet. Thoughts, sounds and movement end when you experience this palpable silence. Initially, you can feel the quietness outside yourself. Then you know the same silence within. You can experience inner peace and an uncomplicated unity between inner and outer. These are precious moments. You can rest in them. They allow the heart to acknowledge the unity of existence.

We can also experience this Oneness in the midst of activity, and these moments often come uninvited. We warm to them. Such experiences may emerge when you are mindful or in an exalted state of awareness. You find yourself responding to them with joyful appreciation, valuing them more than priorities born out of self-interest. It is hard to explain why these moments seem significant, but they do. Any attempt to explain the arising of such experiences seems futile and inappropriate.

In the aftermath of knowing this Oneness, you feel the happiness of being alive. This feeling of unity gives you the sense of co-operating with what is healthy. You notice that such divine experiences arise more easily and frequently. You know a deep sense of belonging, not an isolated belonging to a family or nation, but something that expands much further. Every day you feel your presence remains intimately connected with the presence of everyone and everything else. Such experiences will lift you out of the perceptions of your conventional self.

Whether we feel Oneness in the midst of activity or in the quietness of the night, there is something more than just the experience itself. The appreciation of its place in the scheme of things is important too. We can experience a different sense of things altogether, one in which we can see, in a remarkable way, that time and space lack the ultimate significance that we attribute to these two elements.

Oneness gives a sense of harmony and unity. Our self and all that we relate to in time and space are supported in this experience of Oneness. We owe it to ourselves to step out of the known and the familiar and expose ourselves to the unfamiliar. The teacher never regretted his weekend in the Welsh mountains.

# DEPENDENT ARISING

*When we look at a rainbow, we know that it is not a solid,
separate entity: the beautiful colours arise from the interaction
of raindrops and sunlight.*

Old Buddhist texts use the analogy of the chariot to describe a
human being in terms of the coming together of a number of conditions that arise dependently. The chariot consists of many parts.
When we put all the parts together, the chariot performs its function. If we take all the parts apart, it then ceases to be a chariot. The
same principle applies to a human being. We consist of the sum
total of our parts: body, feelings, perceptions, thoughts and consciousness. None of the parts can survive by themselves. They have
no inherent self-existence. All depend on the support of the other
parts. Furthermore, a person cannot exist without the presence of
the world around them. A human being lacks any independent self-
existence. All of these simple, basic truths are worthy of being
meditated on. We can discover much through exploring the significance of all of this.

Another misunderstood word in the 2,500-year-old Buddhist
tradition is the word *emptiness*. Critics view emptiness as life-negat-
ing; a statement that life is purposeless, and a refutation of all
experiences and views. Emptiness is then associated with nihilism.
Although it is frequently translated as 'emptiness', the Sanskrit
word *shunyata* does not imply that at all. It means that everything
is empty of an independent self-existence. Nothing exists by itself.

The existence of the world is due to *dependent arising*, to the
web of connections. Emptiness of the notion of separateness
expresses this understanding. Nothing exists uniquely unto itself

and all things arise dependently. Understanding emptiness is not the negation of the web of existence but the confirmation of it. Emptiness of self-existence makes everything possible. If there were true self-existence then nothing could change, nothing would be affected by anything else.

A 'person' consists of the interrelationship of various interacting conditions. We depend upon the environment for air, water, light, ground to walk on, and so on. We use the language of 'I' and 'you', 'this' and 'that', to designate separate features in existence. The whole process of life reveals that nothing is self-existent.

A rainbow is a clear reminder to us of conditions coming together and dissolving. When we look at a rainbow, we know that it is not a solid, separate entity: the beautiful colours arise from the interaction of raindrops and sunlight. Yet in conventional language we say, 'What a wonderful rainbow!' as if it were separate and substantial. We relate to the self in the same way when we say, 'What a beautiful person!' People and rainbows belong together interdependently in the vast web of existence.

A deep appreciation of dependently arising conditions acts as a catalyst for the heart to open. We can experience daily the underlying interrelatedness of all 'things'. We can lose the habit of imposing *thingness* on the appearance of particulars. We can let go of our belief that we need to uphold separateness, division and conflict. We can lose interest in perceiving millions of separate and self-existing things. Ego and the world of separate and different things go together: the two are mutually dependent. This world makes us what we are and we make the world what it is. Ego clings to *things,* and *things* that are clung to make the ego.

Nobody is condemned to perceive the world as consisting exclusively of self, other selves and things, and nothing else. It only takes one flash of insight to change our way of looking at the world. When we genuinely understand the emptiness of the view of self and separate things, compassion arises because we see the pain of the self that is caught up in beliefs around separation and clinging. Our pain is no longer our own; it is related to the pain of all human beings. The pain out there and the pain within are not different, not separate. The wisdom of the heart cannot turn its back on the manifestation of suffering for the fictional reality of 'me, me, me'.

Let us not concern ourselves with notions of a substantial self in a world of substantial items. Let us be unshakeably aware that everything relates to everything else. We will look at profit and loss, praise and blame, victory and defeat, health and sickness, pleasure and pain in a different light. We can be at peace with what is rather than caught up in fears and hopes.

If all is here, you are here. If you are here, then all is here. When we intuitively understand the Emptiness of any inherent self-existence, we realise we abide selflessly in this unfolding process. Such realisation brings transcendent joy.

# BABA'S WILL?

*Obeying a guru's command to drop the intellect often
means submitting to their authority instead.*

Some people who were seeking enlightenment began to recognise
the limitations of their own efforts to become liberated. They met
a guru who told them, 'Everything is in the hands of Baba (God).'
They attended numerous 'darshans' with the kindly guru, and
began to adopt his view. They believed that there was absolutely
nothing they could do: whatever happened to them, ordinary or
super-ordinary, rested in the hands of Baba. They no longer took
any responsibility for their actions, good, bad or indifferent. They
saw themselves as puppets in the hands of the Puppeteer. They
believed they had let go of their intellect, and began to promote the
message of the guru: 'Baba makes all decisions. Your mind belongs
to Baba.' It seemed an easy way out of the difficult decisions that
arise in anyone's life.

Their guru told some of his followers to go back to the West,
get a job and start a family, although it wasn't what they felt appropriate for them at this time in their life. Rather than make their own
decisions, they blindly followed the views of their guru. 'It's Baba's
will,' they said. Some of their friends applauded them for following the will of God, but others felt they had handed over their free
spirits to a guru with questionable views.

Some people who pursue religious experience in the Eastern
traditions react against the use of thought. Some gurus tell their
followers: 'Let go of your mind.' This is an interesting idea! Is it
possible? It seems rather impractical. This approach indicates a
negative reaction to thinking. If adopted, this idea leads to all kinds
of confusion. Obeying a guru's command to drop the intellect often
means submitting to their authority instead.

It is necessary to reflect clearly and critically to know the difference between wisdom and submission. People give the authority figure authority as a way of escaping dealing with the consequences of taking decisions for themselves. It is so much easier to hand all responsibility over to the guru. There is no room for doubt in such a mind. What is it that goes unexamined in such views? Firstly, Baba, or God, has no true existence. Baba is merely a concept in the mind charged with feelings and energy. Secondly, such views leave believers in a childlike and submissive role. Such a belief system attracts minds that wish to transfer all power on to another.

It is all too easy in the West to take a disparaging view of such beliefs. Most of us have made 'I' and 'my' our God, and react furiously to believers who worship at the feet of a guru, lama or their Deity. We think they have lost their minds, and we may be right. However, we forget that the same principle applies to those who have lost their minds to the demands of the ego embedded in it.

Far too many people believe in reason as a force that can negate beliefs of the heart. Not surprisingly, this leads to conflict between the rational mind and the emotional life. The rational mind may be correct, and point out in a reasonable way how illogical beliefs in Baba are, and all the limitations of such a standpoint, but it will rarely sway the believer. Their heart matters more to them than intellectual correctness.

We know the tree by its fruits. A mango tree produces sweet fruit and a neem tree bitter fruit. What manifests in our life matters most. If belief in Baba (whether Baba exists or not) produces wisdom and compassion, then that needs to be recognised. Other people may think that this belief is founded on a questionable basis. If the belief collapses, the love and compassion may be transformed into personal crisis and daily despair. An awakened life generates love without depending on beliefs in a supernatural being. It is the love that counts.

# DOING GOOD

*Some people ridicule those who do good. They talk behind their back and make snide remarks. Such people often have pleasure and self-interest as their most desirable goals.*

The wife of an Asian heart-specialist had a serious heart disease. Her husband had the skills and expertise to perform the delicate operation. He wanted to do it more than anything else, but he could not: he wasn't sure he had the confidence to perform the long operation on his wife. The thought of operating on her made him feel nervous. He decided not to operate himself, but instead to direct his assistant as he performed the surgery. His wife died on the operating table. The surgeon never knew whether he should have performed the intricate skills of the operation himself. He was left a widower and in much anguish.

We have to be aware of where our actions are beneficial and where they are harmful. In the surgeon's case, there was no deliberate intention to cause harm, and the outcome of the operation could have gone in any direction. However, the surgeon felt that his inability to operate caused the ultimate harm to his wife. It gave him little comfort to know that his wife might well have died on the operating table even if he had operated. He would have blamed himself for that as well.

We take risks to develop what is healthy and overcome what is harmful. To practise doing good purifies the mind and shows wisdom at work. Sometimes we are not totally sure of what is the right thing to do. We can keep acting from healthy motives or we can keep acting from unhealthy ones, or from a mixture of the two. Our motivations act as a centre around which many other mental states collect and form.

Some people ridicule those who do good. They talk behind

their back and make snide remarks. Such people often have plea-sure and self-interest as their most desirable goals: people who do good make them feel uncomfortable. Acts of goodness contribute directly to the happiness and peace of mind of the beneficiary. Such acts reveal a truly cultured and evolved human being, who is will-ing to sacrifice self-interest for the sake of others. If our life fails to measure up to such noble ways of living, then we ought to make the effort to associate with those who devote their lives to acts of good-ness. Perhaps their goodness will be a source of inspiration for our-selves.

We often express concern about what we see on television or read in the newspaper. But we do little or nothing about it. Our brief concerns seem very shallow. Do we really feel concern? Deep concern will lead to responsible action, small as that may be in the scheme of things. We may read about, or see on television, suffer-ing in our own country, or terrible things that happen overseas. Our politicians make decisions to wage wars, exploit markets and pursue power. But reading about all this becomes light entertain-ment to fill in time.

Carried to excess, the news becomes a distraction from a life of awareness. If the amount of time we spent reading or watching doc-umentaries, we gave to changing the world, it would be a different place. Like the bushes and plants in our garden, we prune the mind of the extraneous so it can flower to its full potential. Then there is energy for total living. You don't have to create the energy or find the time, only abandon what is not necessary.

We may flatter others when we see their goodness of heart man-ifesting in countless ways. There are people who genuinely express deep goodness in their daily lives. If we are not in contact with such people, then we ought to make it a high priority.

Unless pruned, plants and trees become useless, they grow haphazardly and do not bring forth any real fruit. In the same way if we are to grow, if we are to develop, it is necessary to cut back on superficial preoccupations in order to awaken our lives. To make this noble effort shows love and connection with life. The present and future welfare of life depends on such decisions.

# AUTHENTIC
# KNOWLEDGE

*In authentic knowledge, reason consists in directing sensible
people towards a proper course of action. We can, of course,
reason in a false or misleading way to serve selfish ends.*

Many religions take their scriptural injunctions as the highest
knowledge. To accept scripture as the highest knowledge there
must be an element of faith. Self-interest inflates faith by conclud-
ing that this scripture alone is true, and all else is false. It is essential to ascertain that knowledge based on authority, such as a book
or a tradition, is well recorded, well remembered and true. The
opposite could easily be the case.

Knowledge can also be gained through experiences, the senses,
research and reasoning. For example, we notice an angry person
behaving in an unpleasant way, and that the people around him do
not respect him. From this we can infer, 'If I am an angry type,
people will look down on me, they will keep their distance from me.'
People welcome a considerate person, so if we act in a similar way
we can deduce that others will welcome us. We may also inflate the
significance of these other forms of knowledge through our claims.

Authentic knowledge comes from our own experience, from
what we see, know and comprehend. It is bound to include an element of interpretation, leaving a margin of error in our understanding. Authentic, or spiritual knowledge differs from purely
intellectual knowledge since it transforms our way of living. It
helps us to see with clarity. Experience confirms authentic knowledge. Such knowledge includes

- The relationship between subject and object.

- The use of labels and their impact.
- Tendencies that influence our perceptions.
- Matters of the heart.
- Knowledge of enlightenment.

Direct experience and insight eradicates inner suffering in its various manifestations, and the causes of suffering. Without such first-hand experience, Dharma teachings become a theory, something to believe or disbelieve rather than apply. In authentic knowledge, reason consists in directing sensible people towards a proper course of action. We can, of course, reason in a false or misleading way to serve selfish ends. Reason tells us to examine suffering and its causes, to look at clinging and possessiveness. To ignore the call of such reason seems foolish in the extreme. In times of difficulty, we may remind ourselves to be reasonable. If we subscribe to the habit of always wanting things our way, we become more and more unreasonable. It is vital we consider the impact our actions have on others.

When we exaggerate the importance of reason, we depend more and more upon thought to resolve every issue. We dream up hypothetical situations to cope with anything that sounds unreasonable or fails to fit in with our idea of things. There was a serious-minded Buddhist who enjoyed listening to the teachings, but who regarded them as an intellectual challenge. He had often heard from the teachers about our capacity to live life without fear and worry. To his intellectual way of thinking, such potential seemed unreasonable. His mind would immediately swing into 'what if' mode. What if your house burned down? What if you found out you had terminal cancer? What if your daughter was in a road accident? The intellectual mind cannot imagine handling wisely such calamities without being torn apart through anxiety. At such times, reason must give way to experience, practice and insight. We can experience love and wise action rather than terror and torment. Authentic knowledge makes use of experience, reasoning and wise texts as resources for awakening.

We must understand that true reality is beyond thoughts, beyond the reasoning of the mind. Reason can help to make the ultimate truth possible, but it cannot reveal it. Only direct experience and realisation can do that.

# HOW AND WHY

*Experts always seem to discover new reasons for the fact that we
do not always seem perfectly well . . . We can go into problems of
the past, make changes, and perhaps later find new problems.*

The human spirit does a tremendous amount of investigation. A
lively, energetic mind is constantly seeking to understand cause
and effect. It never remains satisfied with the old answers, but seeks
out different ones. This has led to specialisation in every area of
study and work. We are fascinated by questions that start with
'how' and 'why'. Medicine is the classic example, with eye specialists, ear specialists, skin specialists, heart specialists and so on. We
want to know how to deal with something, and so we look for causes
in the past. We may locate the causes, but it may not make any difference to the effect.

A team of dentists concluded that the metals used for filling
teeth caused physical ills in other parts of the body. The dentists
said that people's meridian energy lines become contaminated
because these metals affect organs, including the liver and kid-
neys. In turn, this affects people's state of mind, generating
moodiness and melancholy. The dentists recommended that all
the old fillings should be removed, and replaced with gold or
expensive porcelain fillings. It sounded reasonable to patients who
saw their brochures and advertisements. Some people believed the
dentists and forked out thousands of pounds to have all their fillings changed.

Experts always seem to discover new reasons for the fact that
we do not always seem perfectly well. But there is no solution that
will produce permanent health since we abide in a world of birth,
ageing, pain and death. We can go into problems of the past, make
changes, and perhaps later find new problems. We can make our-

selves ill trying to protect ourselves from all the conditions that make us ill.

Mental activity is subtler than material activity, and can provide us with greater insights into the laws of nature. It is the microcosm of the macrocosm. In order for something to arise, something else needs previously to have arisen. We need basic knowledge, basic awareness and basic application, otherwise we will spend our lives running around from doctors to dentists, traditional and new age, trying to ensure that every feature of our anatomy runs smoothly. Through wisdom, we respond to the basic needs of the body such as diet, exercise and posture.

Spending too much time obsessing about our body puts a brake on the opportunity to enter the field of expansive awareness, where we have the capacity to embrace the entire field of cause and effect. This field of awareness reveals liberation where we 'know' freedom from bondage to our body.

Due to the particularisation of things by the mind, we grant time and space a reality, and we seem to live in it. Freedom is stepping outside this prison, outside the self's tendency to latch on to particulars. Liberation is comparable to somebody who has been in prison for a long time and then is released.

Once a year, I meet some Palestinians in the city of Nablus on the West Bank. It is part of the ongoing dialogue between Israelis and Palestinians. The brother of one of the participants had spent twenty-seven years in an Israeli jail after participating in the 1967 Arab–Israeli war. One day, his jailers went to his cell unexpectedly, and released him. They walked him to the main entrance of the prison, opened the door, let him out, and locked and bolted the door behind him. He had no idea why the Israeli authorities chose to release him or how he would spend the rest of his life.

He didn't care. He was free. That's all that mattered. Twenty-seven years were behind him. He had no idea what to do or where to go. For that he jumped up in the air with joy and then set off down the road to Nablus to find family and friends.

# IDEALS AND
# THE SELF

*Ultimately it becomes an act of irresponsibility to spend most of
our life involved in the construction of the self and its future
rather than looking deeply into things*

The here and now matters more than the past and future. The
living present serves as an open doorway to understand what it
means to be in this world. We rarely give the present moment the
attention it deserves.

There are many sound reasons to engage in spiritual practices
in order to experience fully the here and now. Such practices can
help us feel centred; to indulge less in memories and plans; to know
we are in touch with something, not just living in fantasies. Being
in the here and now harnesses our energies, so that we feel a steadfast purpose in all our activities.

In being present in the present, we are much more receptive to
the bare data that comes to our ears, eyes, nose, tongue and body.
We can respond to it in a clear and unconfined way. Being in the
here and now is not a superficial thing: it is one of the guiding prin-
ciples of wise living. The here and now is an open doorway to
knowing and understanding the nature of things, but it would be an
error of judgement to make it an end in itself.

There are those who endeavour to dismiss spiritual practices
that prioritise the present moment. They think they are a way of
avoiding long-term responsibility. They may be right from a conventional standpoint, but ultimately it becomes an act of irresponsibility to spend most of our life involved in the construction of the
self and its future rather than looking deeply into things.

Whatever we commit ourselves to can have benefits and

dangers. When we are solidly present, we feel our practice is becoming firmly established. We feel content. But once we have embraced this ideal of being grounded in the here and now, we experience its opposite – not being here and now. This seems grossly unfair, but commitment to a certain experience naturally makes us aware of times when we are not feeling it. We find ourselves being present and not being present, and unless we understand the dangers of being goal-oriented in our spiritual practice, we can find ourselves satisfied when we are present and dissatisfied when we are not.

When we set up ideals to attain in our spiritual practice, we are supporting notions of success and failure, progress and regress. No matter how noble these ideals are, they build up a sense of self in the form of the achiever or underachiever. The sense of 'I' is substantiated every time we become caught up in our interpretation of results, whether pleasing or displeasing. As long as we continue to view our practice like this, the result is tied to self.

We know from Buddhist teachings, or our own firsthand experience, that liberation reveals the fiction of the self. It is an enormous challenge to question the authenticity of the self, to witness the way it manipulates events. We are often more interested in improving the self than in letting it go. What would it mean to give up all features of the ambitious self and experience life fully without that construction? There would be nothing for us to demand from the world, nor pursue for our own ends. The manner of our relationships would be different, since we would no longer be in pursuit of attention and favours. The notion of accumulating experiences, possessions, power and privilege would seem irrelevant.

There would be a freedom that remained steady amidst daily circumstances. We would go about our business in a different way. If we gave up all features of the ambitious self, there would be nothing to gain or lose at any level. There would be not only a sublime joy; we would know an enlightened life.

# Stay Awake!

---

*The reason things happen to us is because our actions were
probably geared towards them. If we really get a sense of what
this means, and how our mind is the governing factor of our
whole life, we begin to see our destiny.*

We suffer when we don't want to experience what we find ourselves going through. Suffering is the wish to be free from something that is taking place within us. It takes the form of stress,
unhappiness, confusion, selfishness – the whole repertoire of words
that we have to describe the state of not feeling free.

Without awareness, we are unable to see the seeds we sow, nor
accommodate the fruits that inevitably follow. We can't understand how we came to be unhappy, sad or confused, because some-
how we missed all the signs, both subtle and obvious, that would
have shown us what had been going on in our lives. If we remain
attentive, we'll pick up the signals, and notice what our mind is
doing. We'll know when it is caught up in wanting and clinging to
things.

Paying attention to life can protect us from suffering. If we
really notice the movements of our minds, we will be alert throughout the day, and take a natural interest in each situation. We will be
committed to learn from our experiences whether pleasurable or
painful. That commitment gives purpose to our lives. There will be
a lot more happiness in our lives as a result of our ability to make
difficult decisions and learn from the consequences. We get ourselves into a mess through indecision. Our indecisiveness then
escalates into thinking that we have major decisions to make. Our
wavering creates the size of the decision, not the other way around.

I remember giving evening talks on decision-making on a
retreat. I made a comment, almost as an aside, that the major

decision of life has already been made. Right after the talk and for the next day or two, retreatants approached me to ask what I meant by the remark. I had had nothing esoteric in mind. All the people on that ten-day retreat had made the decision to explore and practise the Dharma. There is nothing more important for each individual and for life on earth. I believe all other decisions must fit into that major decision. The Dharma will protect those who protect it.

Every event is raw material for insight, for spiritual practice. When an unexpected event happens, it can collide with the habit patterns in our mind and we feel pain. The pain is saying, 'Wake up!' We thought everything was fine and that we were doing all right. When we get into a mess, we realise that we were asleep all along and had deceived ourselves into thinking that we were awake. Any suffering we experience shows us that we aren't awake. If we were, we wouldn't be in this condition. That's why the teachings say repeatedly, please stay awake. Stay awake!

You get what you deserve, but mostly you get what you ask for. If you really look closely at any situation, you can see that you probably contributed as much as anybody else – even the suffering, the pain, the difficulty and the hardships. The reason things happen to us is because our actions were probably geared towards them. If we really get a sense of what this means, and how our mind is the governing factor of our whole life, we begin to see our destiny.

Right now, we might not see the direction of our lives because our mind moves backwards and forwards over so many issues. We can't see the main current. When the mind becomes more centred, we find the current that finds its way to the ocean. We begin to know its flow from the past through the present and into the future. If you know the past and the present, you can sense the future. The mind will generate signals for encouragement and for vigilance. There may be unforeseen fruits that dramatically change things, but for the most part, we can see the direction of our lives.

We have the potential to experience daily the fullness of things whether we engage in doing or not doing. If we engage in action and there is a gain, it should make no difference to that sense of fullness we feel. If we engage in action and there is a loss or a mistake, that should make no difference to it either. If we neither engage in action nor look for results, fullness still abides. Moreover, we know it. Gain or loss is cancelled out in that fullness.

In the fullness of things, there is a sense of wonder that is our birthright to know.

Contemplation, awareness, meditation, insight and understanding are all about knowing that fullness so that it is abundantly clear, regardless of events. The fullness of things ought to be self-evident. If we are blessed, we can sense the fullness for ourselves. We don't need anyone to confirm it. That's why the sages say repeatedly there is nothing to be done. Everything is full and complete already. Not surprisingly, their single, core message is: 'Stay awake!'

# THE DISCOVERY
# OF LIBERATION

# THE SEEKER AND
# THE SOUGHT

*We already are what we are seeking. Until we realise this, we
will never find peace of mind, nor awaken to the totality
of things.*

One of the best-loved stories in the non-dual teachings of Mother
India concerns the 'Tenth Man'. Ten men set off to swim across
the River Ganges. When they got to the other side of the river, one
of the men decided to count everybody up to make sure that all had
swum safely across to the other side. The man could only find nine
others. He began searching for the Tenth Man. He split them up
into groups but he only counted six and three, five and four, seven
and two.

A fisherman sitting on the beach repairing his fishing net
pointed to the seeker and said to him, 'You are the Tenth Man.
The seeker is the sought.' At that point, the Tenth Man woke up.
We imagine we will find what we seek outside ourselves, and wan-
der here and there in a forlorn search for satisfaction and solutions.
We already are what we are seeking. Until we realise this, we will
never find any peace of mind, nor awaken to the totality of things.

The story of the Tenth Man points out the significance of the
seeker. Once found, the totality of things embraces the seeker and
the sought equally. Until then, we live as though we are separate
from everything and everyone else. Forgetting to include ourselves, we find ourselves running into problems and seeking for
answers.

Let us examine the seeker. You are a seeker looking for something. You are looking for real satisfaction at the material, physical,
emotional, intellectual or spiritual level. Your life has become a

constant search. This is true of the mind of every conditioned person. You may live in the fantasy that the future will produce a better situation than the present, but the future is a mere modification of the present, not the secret hiding place of what you seek.

Yet you still go on chasing the phantom treasure, believing that the future hides it. No matter how often you accomplish a goal a new one pops up in its place. Why do you ignore the option of paying full attention to the one person who really matters to you – yourself? Who are you before the seeker and the sought arises in your mind? The seeker is in bondage to the sought.

We may retort that if we stop seeking, life loses all meaning. It dawned clearly upon the Tenth Man that his seeking obscured reality. Though you may not fathom it out, everything is here already. There is nothing to add to this fulfilment. The seeker and the sought belong to a misunderstanding, a foolish belief that there is a gap between who we are and what we are looking for. The sought blinds us to the seeker and the seeker blinds us to the sought. Knowing the emptiness of the seeker and the sought dissolves both.

Then there is no more distortion in the mind. Everything rests in its original nature. There is an immediately available reality that remains steady and undisturbed. The seeker and the sought obscure the underlying nature of things that remain unaffected by seeking. It is simple misunderstanding to live in the world of self and other, and the endless short-lived successes and failures that unite the two.

In this bare reality, stripped of all pretensions, our search is fulfilled. The fiction of seeking has ended. We experience the timeless wonder and mystery emerging through the non-dual. The Tenth Man reveals himself equally everywhere.

# A WAVE IN
# THE OCEAN

*Sometimes we seem to be going against the whole range of
religious beliefs when we dismiss the notion of God. It seems
easier to go along with set beliefs rather than trying to point
out other ways of understanding our lives on this earth.*

All things change. Whatever you see, hear or think about changes
its form and character and becomes something different. This
'becoming' is everywhere and in everything. Conventional existence reveals nothing that we can confirm as permanent. The
moment that just passed was different from this present moment,
and this present moment will not be the same as the next. There is
no permanent self, no essence, no creator of this process, no
Supreme Being. When we witness things as a dependently arising
process, it can seem very cold and impersonal, but this reveals a
fixed attitude of mind rather than a connection with the dynamic
and awesome movement of existence that reveals neither beginning
nor end.

Sometimes we seem to be going against the whole range of religious beliefs when we dismiss the notion of God. It seems easier to
go along with set beliefs rather than trying to point out other ways
of understanding our lives on this earth. In Egypt, they say if you
see the town worshipping a cow, then mow the grass and feed it. In
other words, it's not worth the hassle of standing apart.

At times, we feel helplessly swept along in the great rush of life.
We might like to comfort ourselves that all beings are moving
towards the same supreme goal at different rates, but as a viewpoint, this is hard to prove. We might draw the conclusion that all
forms of life, sentient and insentient, are helplessly caught up in the

great movement of life. We might conclude that there is no way out, no release, but this too would be another viewpoint. However, wisdom teachings and realisation point to a way out of this apparently hopeless situation. Awakening shows that we are not trapped in this movement from birth to death.

Like all phenomena, we manifest a beginning and an end. From birth to death, the dance of becoming goes on – a cell becomes a foetus, then a child, an adult, middle-aged, old and dust. At the mental level, there is the arising of various states of mind, deep and shallow. People frequently become fooled by their mental states, believing them to be an accurate barometer of themselves. As a result different notions arise about 'who I am', 'who I was', or 'what I will be'.

We believe that who we are in any moment is the aspect of mind and body we are currently identifying with. However, there is no evidence whatsoever to suggest that we are the function of what we identify with. Whatever a person has become will pass away. Health and sickness, praise and blame, profit and loss, winning and losing, success and failure belong to the field of becoming. Attaching the self to any one of these conditions generates problems when the condition changes.

We sometimes forget that to go deep into ourselves corresponds with going deep into the field of existence, since we are not separate from everything else. There is much to be discovered when we find ourselves in meditation deeper than our thoughts. In such depths of meditation, we find our perceptions alter. The ego and demands of the self make less impact on our relationship to events.

We are all like waves rising and falling on the surface of the ocean, and when the wave looks deep within, it finds the ocean. When we do not hold on to the past, cherish the future or take hold of the present, we see imperturbability. In spite of the constant change in all appearances, there is nothing special in the waves of the ocean of cosmic life. The ocean is grounded in imperturbability, and the dance of the waves radiates joy.

# A FLEA IN
# THE MIND

*That is just how it is with the ego: it's imaginary.*
*It is empty of any true existence; we cannot lay our hands*
*on it since it has no colour, sound or shape, yet we act*
*as if it is really something substantial.*

There is a story from the East that demonstrates the unreality of
the ego. The story tells of a man convinced that a flea wandered
around inside his head. He was extremely concerned. The flea
crawled over his brain, down the back and sides of his head. He met
wise people who told him, 'Look, there's no flea. You have to
understand. There is no flea there.' The worried man said, 'I've
had this flea for as long as I can remember. I can feel it. I can
experience it. Don't tell me that there is no flea. There IS a flea.'
And they said, 'No, no, no. It's all in your imagination.' He even
had X-rays, but ignored their findings, since they were the same as
everybody else's.

Finally, the man came to a wise Buddhist teacher who applied
the solution of *upaya*. (This is a Sanskrit word that means skilful,
that is, knowing the way to liberation.) The wise man said, 'Aha,
yes! You've got a flea.' The worried man expressed enormous
relief: 'At last somebody believes me. I'm not a fool. I do have a flea
in my head.'

The wise man said to the man with the flea, 'I have some medicine, made by the Pleasant Street Drug Company. If you take this
medicine for fourteen days, the flea will come out of your ear.' The
man took the medicine and fourteen days later returned to the wise
man. The wise man secretly got out a matchbox with a flea inside,
and put the matchbox to the man's ear. He told the man to tilt his

head over to one side: 'Ah, here's the flea. Look, it has come out.' The man felt overwhelmed with gratitude. He no longer had to worry about the flea. He felt clear, content and untroubled.

That is just how it is with the ego: it's imaginary. It is empty of any true existence; we cannot lay our hands on it since it has no colour, sound or shape, yet we act as if it is really something substantial. We therefore apply *upaya*, employing imaginary techniques to get rid of an imaginary issue. It's an extraordinary game, yet seems to have a serious note. There is no point in treating either the ego or the technique as substantial, since both belong to imaginary existence.

Perhaps one of the best-known resources for working directly on the flea in the mind is meditation – a resource for insight, as well as calmness and relaxation. Formal sitting and walking meditations can be used not only to still the mind, but also to see into it. To see with clarity, to walk with clarity, to hear with clarity requires formal practice. We can't tell our mind to stay clear, focused and awake, as the mind won't take any notice whatsoever. That's the flea doing the telling. We bring the light of awareness to the movement of the mind, noticing the way the flea gets into relationship with our body, emotions, perceptions, thoughts and even into awareness itself.

Meditation gives us the opportunity to know what it means to live without the flea affecting our lives, or only flitting around occasionally. We can see clearly where satisfaction and dissatisfaction come from, and observe the relationship both have to the ego. Ego activity easily gets caught up in the dualities of mind – likes and dislikes, wanting and rejecting, attraction and aversion. The flea makes the mind itch. Thinking, thinking, thinking seems much like scratching an itch – a temporary relief – but then the itch starts again.

Stability in the mind effortlessly reveals the disturbances that end in agitation, worry and selfish demands. We track the flea until it has exhausted itself. The itch in the mind is over: there is no greater release.

# SUBJECT AND OBJECT

*The movement of attraction or aversion fixes an object in our mind, consolidates it, and then makes its importance concrete.*

Our mind is continuously moving in two major, opposing directions. One is the movement towards pleasant things that we feel attracted to, and the other is movement away, pulling back from unpleasant situations. We can spend our life trapped in these two forces of attraction and aversion without ever examining our psychological imprisonment. Stuck in habitual and addictive patterns, we can find ourselves helplessly pulled towards certain objects and fleeing from others.

In the conventional view of reality, our mind *is* a movement in the field of time, so it is hardly surprising that we continuously find ourselves moving towards and away from things. If we look further, we discover that this movement of the mind (the subject) in relation to a person, situation, place, or thing (the object) actually establishes our relationship to the world. Objects establish the condition of the subject (the sense of 'I'), and the subject establishes the view of the object.

The movement of attraction or aversion fixes an object in our mind, consolidates it, and then makes its importance concrete. In this way we, the subject, influence the way the object appears. We do not see the object clearly because we do not discriminate between its basic characteristics and those that we project upon it. The movement of our own mind adds characteristics to the object that it does not intrinsically possess; builds it up; and makes it seem more than it actually is. The more the mind moves, the more significance, value, and importance the object takes on.

So we must ask the question: 'Is the object anything by itself without the subject?' The constant movement of the mind not only affects the object but also establishes the subject, the 'I'. Subject and object keep reinforcing each other. For example, I am a son (subject) and I keep thinking about my father (object). Subject confirms object and object confirms subject. There is a state of mind fixing subject and object. Desire and rejection, praise and blame distort both subject and object. We forget that the *thought* of our father is not our father.

When the mind is in a state of great movement, the object seems radically different from the subject. We act as if the object stood truly endowed with the features that we project on to it. This sense of self and other is created through the actual movement of the mind. With greater steadiness of mind and inner stillness, the apparently enormous difference between self and other gradually lessens. It then becomes possible to see things in a completely different way.

We can practise steadying our mind and becoming aware of the movements as they occur. We begin to see when we are moving towards something or someone and when we are avoiding or moving away from them. Although there are certainly things that it is necessary to move towards and secure and other things that it is necessary to move away from and avoid, meditation reduces the unnecessary mind-swings that keep us agitated and unbalanced. Meditation grounds and centres the mind so the tipping of the scales up and down, for and against, towards and away from become negligible. There is no substitute for a clear and balanced existence between subject and object.

Through inner stillness, we come to understand how our mind fastens on to things. We learn to let go of the type of events and situations we tend to fixate on. Gradually, we become aware of how our minds invest objects with features that then affect our ability to act wisely. Putting a lot of unwise energy into an object serves nobody. Through clarity, we can acknowledge that objects have no inherent control over our lives. Wisdom is learning to see clearly where we place power and authority. We are no longer compelled to live like cats and dogs, yelping and running after one thing and then yelping and running away from something else with our tails between our legs.

In our old way of perceiving, there was a great difference between subject and object, but now we begin to recognise that the subject and its object are not separate from one another. In fact, they are mutually dependent. The object of thought depends for the way it appears upon the limitations of the sense doors and the condition of the mind. On the other hand, the subject, the thinker, establishes the quality of our relationship. This is true whether the object is in the immediate world; something from the past manifesting as memory; or an object of future expectation.

As the contrast between subject and object is reduced, harmony and oneness become more apparent. In this harmony, the subject and object enter into a beneficial, undemanding relationship. We sense that this is the way things are when we strip thought of desire and projections. It seems ridiculous to believe in the mind-made reality created by pursuit and avoidance.

We are always faced with this duality of subject and object. Life is based on this relationship of oneself as the subject to something else as the object. The raw material for insight and understanding lies within this activity. To see intuitively into the true nature of things, we need to embrace the Immeasurable that contains subject and object.

# FREEDOM FROM MOMENTARY CONDITIONS

*It is not only freedom to and freedom from that can be discovered, but unconditional freedom amidst the appearance of momentary conditions.*

In meditation there is the power to develop microscopic seeing. I have mentioned several times the importance of witnessing moment-to-moment change. Our entire cellular existence changes subtly every moment of our lives. We need to practise living in tune with this actuality if we want to eliminate the problems associated with clinging to continuity or fear of change.

It is possible to witness the dissolution of what appears as it appears moment to moment. This demonstrates the power of the mind to know and experience its momentary condition. The mind may loosen up considerably when you focus deeply like this. Such experiences remind us of the absurdity of trying to hold on to anything.

It is not unusual for the sincere meditator to restrict their field of meditation to a narrow witnessing of impermanence at a subtle level. Such microscopic seeing acts as a step along the way. After becoming disillusioned with clinging to notions of continuity, it is natural to want to dissolve all attachments.

One woman had sat a total of more than twenty-two Vipassana (Insight Meditation) courses, each lasting for ten days. She had been taught by a follower of a Burmese Buddhist tradition, who told his students that after three ten-day courses they had to commit themselves to using only that method, and nothing else. They were not allowed to go elsewhere, or listen to other teachers. Their goal seemed to be developing equanimity in the face of witnessing impermanence at the moment-to-moment level. She was told that if she sat a retreat with another teacher she would not be allowed back. She came to meet me secretly. She was experiencing doubts about being tied to this method, which is known as 'sweeping', since practitioners do nothing but move their attention from head to foot as a 'practice for purification'. She had tried for the last three courses to 'sweep away her doubts' without success.

I told the woman she was right to listen to her doubts. As with many things, benefits can carry a sting in the tail. We place a value on something, invest in it and create a hierarchy of experience. Like the woman, we may be told we can only practise one method, that to explore further would be like digging lots of little holes and never going deep enough to find oil. We believe what we are told, so we focus on simply witnessing impermanence, for example, even though we never reach the oil. We lose sight of liberation because we are clinging to the continuity of a single method. It is easy to be so caught up with the means that we lose sight of the end.

We must learn to trust ourselves to make our own choices. To discover the immeasurable, we must learn to live in a spacious way. This goes further than microscopic seeing: we do not feel so encumbered, narrow or limited, and since the spacious element is formless, the mind–body process begins to lose some of its solidity. We realise that we do not have to dissolve mind–body and consciousness, or let it go. We do not have to get rid of anything to know reality. The mind–body – the movement and non–movement of mind – does not hinder seeing. If we can live in full acknowledgement of all things, we can know what it means to be liberated here and now.

There are times in the meditative journey when all that we experience is space. The sense of space becomes so established that we can become deeply absorbed within it. As phenomena keep presenting themselves, they do not impinge, obstruct or deny that element in any way. Spaciousness is not fulfilment, but provides an opportunity for liberating understanding through the heart's expansion within it. What matters is knowing freedom.

We are free to observe, free to act and to express freedom from fear. It is not only freedom *to* and freedom *from* that can be discovered, but unconditional freedom amidst the appearance of momentary conditions. This freedom embraces life itself, and the sense of it is close at hand. At times, we intuitively feel an emancipation that allows us to let go of giving priority to continuity or discontinuity, permanence or impermanence. There is truly no hindrance to this freedom at any moment in life, and the fruit of that freedom is love.

# COMPASSION AND
# LIBERATION

*There can be a real and immediate liberation. An enlightened
person sees through the fiction of the self and the mythology
surrounding it. They know freedom's presence in their daily life
and at the same time are conscious of the circumstances of others.*

Someone I have known for several years came to see me at home.
He told me he was now fully liberated. He had participated in a
number of retreats and workshops, and engaged in intensive meditation. Some weeks previously he had had an experience of going
beyond mind and body, and ever since, he had felt liberated and
enlightened. This liberation was still with him and he felt he was
living in the present moment all the time. When I asked him how
he was living his life since this event, he laughed and said he was
spending time with friends, watching videos into the early hours,
and feeling light, free and happy. Hanging out watching videos
every night seems superficial in the extreme, I told him. How long
will it be before you become bored with such a daily life? He
shrugged, and left. I never saw him again.

A day or two later another friend, a woman dedicated to serving others, came to see me. She had made numerous personal sac-
rifices to sustain her work with victims of child abuse. She had also
participated in several retreats for inner renewal. I noticed she had
a great deal of personal calm and a warm love of others. She said, 'I
serve others and work hard on myself. Instead of taking holidays, I
attend retreats. But I'm not liberated. I'm not an enlightened
human being. I haven't had such an experience.'

I reflected on these two conversations. Both people were talking about themselves in opposite ways. One felt he was enlight-

177

ened. There was nothing more for him to do, nothing more to be gained, and no need to make any further effort. The other felt she was a long way from enlightenment, yet clearly and directly manifested love, concern, and conviction. To whom does our heart respond, despite their different descriptions of themselves?

There can be a real and immediate liberation. An enlightened person sees through the fiction of the self and the mythology surrounding it. They know freedom's presence in their daily life and at the same time are conscious of the circumstances of others. It is a misunderstanding to think that liberation is a short-lived experience followed by an easy way of living. Some claim such enlightenment, but our perception of them makes us feel uncomfortable. It is appropriate to assume that the quality of a liberated person's life will communicate something different to us. Not surprisingly, we tend to doubt the understanding of claimants to enlightenment who seem indifferent to other people.

Some people freely and generously express love, but don't describe themselves as liberated. It may mean they have more work to do on themselves. Perhaps they need a teacher and teachings that point to immediate liberation. On the other hand, perhaps they cling to a picture of what an enlightenment experience is. We must be honest with ourselves and each other when making important statements about who we are. We can deceive ourselves either way.

It is too much to ask the human spirit to be liberated *and* engaged in dedicated service to others? It is not surprising that some teachings seem to neglect the fate of the world. Genuine liberation has an impact on the heart; it brings something deep out of us. Throughout the year, I listen in and out of retreats to people's accounts of their deepest experiences. People say they are liberated, yet an unquenchable love fails to manifest out of that liberation. Others say, 'I am not liberated,' and yet show a tremendous capacity to love.

Perhaps how we think about ourselves doesn't matter so much. One person's thought says: 'I am liberated'. Another person's thought says: 'I am not liberated'. If we can just see the true emptiness of all thoughts about the self, and not cling to any of them, perhaps true liberation is immediately available. Enlightenment still takes place in this world for women and men. It takes place in retreats and monasteries and outside them. The here and now still provides the most wonderful opportunity of all.

The enlightenment of humanity goes on. Through such awakening, we pay the greatest respect to the ordinary and everyday.

# MADE IN OUR IMAGE

*What omniscient God would give powers to human beings to inflict so much suffering on each other, as well as other sentient beings?*

There is a child inside us: a child who wants to surrender to an archetypal parent and who wants a system to follow that will make life easier. We want to be neatly protected from everything so that we don't have to live with our eyes open. There are plenty of religious messages that appeal to the child inside, but genuine inquiry appeals to the adult within us.

To imagine that everything is in the hands of a mythological figure called God, who is above all worldly affairs, cuts us off from living in the real world. For if this is true, God must take total responsibility for all the obscene and barbaric behaviour that runs through human existence. This God is not worthy of worship, not worthy of submission to, but only fit for condemnation. We do not have to seek God's forgiveness for what human beings have inflicted on each other. We need the capacity to forgive God for the pain and sorrow He has permitted to be inflicted on this earth. If we keep praying to God and He doesn't answer our prayers, then perhaps we need to look elsewhere for the answer.

Some religious traditions take a slightly more pragmatic view. They claim there is a God who made us in His image, but God kept some powers for Himself and gave some power to human beings. What would be considered good and beautiful belongs to God, while human beings produce all the suffering that arises on the earth. God also finds Himself left in the most unacceptable condition. What omniscient God would give powers to human beings to inflict so much suffering on each other, as well as other sentient beings?

It is hard to believe that God created the earth, made a laboratory out of it, and watched a tragic experiment of suffering unfold beyond imagination. To non-believers, this God seems powerless to stop His experiment. It would seem an enormous error of judgement on the part of this God to grant independent powers to human beings, knowing their capacity to abuse such powers in the most unimaginably cruel ways. To believe in this God as all-powerful means that we would need to preserve a Hell for one Person, and that Person would be God. We do not need to love this God but to pity Him for a crazy initiative that sadly got out of hand.

There are other religious traditions on the earth who claim God sent down his Son(s) to share in the suffering of others, to know their pain. Others claim that He sent prophets and saints down to earth. To question whether these things actually happened can bring the wrath of believers firmly down upon us. In Dharma teachings, such beliefs are regarded as a metaphor, an interpretation of events. In Dharma, we interpret the metaphor of the Son as meaning that out of realisation of the Immeasurable emerges the compassionate heart.

When we adopt narrow beliefs, we can end up unquestioningly believing in the personality of a deeply compassionate being such as Jesus Christ, and take less and less notice of what he actually said. We disregard his teachings of love, non-harming and voluntary simplicity. Instead, we raise his status to a supernatural level to avoid applying his teachings to our daily life. Religious people can believe in their God, seek the intervention of his Son, prophets or gurus and simultaneously live a life that bears little relationship to their teachings. We want to get as much as we can out of this world for ourselves, family and country, and believe we will go straight into eternal happiness in the next.

Our beliefs easily govern and determine our relationships with people. If we hold on to religious beliefs, we can become intolerant of people who hold different beliefs to our own. If we hold on to secular beliefs, we can become intolerant of people who hold on to religious beliefs. Yet both groups of people have more in common than what separates them. Due to our interpretation of our experience and what we have heard, we draw conclusions which may inhibit an open relationship with others if we look at them through the distortion of our beliefs.

When you put a religious belief on a pedestal, you lose touch with the reality of other people. You have found something to believe in, so you believe others need the same beliefs as you. No wonder many non-believers are cynical about religion. Dharma teachings and practices point to a middle ground neither caught up in extreme beliefs such as an all-powerful God nor thinking that everything rests in the hands of humanity. Nothing is that simple. Claims about what the ultimate truth about the world is remain claims, no more, no less. We can carry on blindly holding on to our beliefs, or examine them to see them for what they are. Beliefs take second place to wisdom.

# THE DANCE
# OF SHIVA

*We can see that what is happening at our sense doors is simply a series of momentary activities and momentary impressions. What we make of these momentary impressions shapes our happiness and unhappiness.*

Indian spirituality has always had a love of the ascetic and austere. The saints and sages have examined the world of pleasure, dismissed the importance of impressions upon the senses, and broadcast an uncompromising message of renunciation. To the Western mind, stories of naked fakirs and sadhus sound bizarre, but it would be a pity to dismiss Indian spirituality out of hand. The sadhus see pleasure- and profit-seekers as equally bizarre and unworldly, since death makes a mockery of all pursuit of privilege and pleasure.

The image of the god Shiva reminds us in tough terms of the life of renunciation. There are many depictions of Shiva, the auspicious one: he is one of the aspects of existence, representing the whole dance of life, the totality of activity and expression. Pictures of Shiva show deep insight: he is depicted virtually naked with long matted hair, and around him is a cobra. The way sadhus mat their hair involves putting wet cow dung on it and then covering it with ashes to dry it out. Despite the danger of the cobra, the repulsiveness of the wet cow dung on his hair and body, having no clothing and being an ascetic, Shiva is dancing.

Such an image may repulse you. You may not be able to relate to it in any way. It seems to confirm all the negative views about Indian spirituality. No Westerner is likely to go out looking for the cow dung to mat their hair. Nevertheless, it would be a pity to dismiss the story of Shiva as many do, including millions of religious

Indians, who find such a lifestyle all a bit strange. We forget the message; Shiva is dancing. Shiva is always dancing. It is the dance of triumph, of joy, of celebration – despite the cobra, the stink of cow dung in his hair and the cold wind on his naked body. Shiva is one with the dance of existence. The whole play of life goes on. How many of us dance daily, even with all the comforts we have surrounded ourselves with?

We can see that what is happening at our sense doors is simply a series of momentary activities and momentary impressions. What we make of these momentary impressions shapes our happiness and unhappiness. When we come down to the actuality, there is a bare touch on the eye in the form of a colour or shape, a bare touch on the ear in the form of a sound, and so on. Present to the eye or ear, present to the mind. These momentary impressions have become very important to us: they make up our world, and it's the only world we know. We can easily find that our time is devoted to experiencing certain types of impressions on our senses and avoiding other impressions.

We can gain some understanding about ourselves from watching the forces of attraction and aversion around these impressions. If we don't, we are liable to get caught up in unhealthy patterns – always wanting things to go our way and hating it when they don't. Sometimes it is hard to admit how much we depend on experiencing pleasant impressions and reacting against unpleasant ones.

Perhaps we have had an experience of really wanting something. We did everything possible to get it. We succeeded and we got a thrill out of it. Perhaps we got a succession of thrills – but eventually the thrill fades. There is no longer excitement, no longer the big buzz that we remember. In retrospect, we often see that the years spent in the pursuit of personal pleasure can feel like wasted time. There are more important things in life than that.

If we can really get a sense of what it means to live fully amidst the sweet and stinking aromas of life, we can become one with Shiva, one with the whole dance of existence.

# A PROFOUND
# OPENING

*We have had a taste of freedom, but then it's gone and we
are left with the memory. We don't feel that depth of freedom
any more so, naturally enough, we would like to repeat
the experience.*

We believe that there's something obstructing unconditional freedom, and when we come down to it we are convinced that states of
mind have an inherent power to stop it. We speak of hindrances,
obstacles, problems, other people, and situations. We've granted all
of these extraordinary powers over our consciousness. We're convinced that people and circumstances block our freedom. We live
in this myth, and we can't imagine it being otherwise. If something
is troubling our mind, we think we must get rid of it or overcome
it, and that once we finish with it, we'll be free. This is a terrible
paradox. Can we hear ourselves saying that the condition for
unconditioned freedom is changing the conditions?

Can our state of mind really block freedom? There may be
some moments when there's a personal story going on in our mind.
We seem caught up in it even though we would rather not have to
go through such an experience, but at the same time we know it is
a state of mind that has arisen and will pass away. If a state of mind
had the power to stay without change, then we would really have a
problem, but this is obviously not the case.

Such experiences seem to reinforce the view that clouds truly
have the capacity to stop the sun from shining. But what side of the
sun are we looking from? This is the extraordinary misunderstanding that we find ourselves believing in. We sometimes experience a
touch of freedom that manifests extraordinarily clearly. At that

moment, we sense we have finally arrived, and there is nothing more to do. We cannot add to this experience in any way. The walls of our mind and the definitions of our existence have dropped away. We experience immeasurable, incomparable freedom. We know that we cannot possibly add to such an experience.

Then this liberating experience fades due to the influence of conditions upon our consciousness. The familiar mind is back, reborn into the present moment. We have had a taste of freedom, but then it's gone and we are left with the memory. We don't feel that depth of freedom any more so, naturally enough, we would like to repeat the experience. Should that be our priority?

A profound opening can have an extraordinary impact on our perceptions and priorities. There are two ways to acknowledge such a deep experience. You can recognise the experience for itself with appreciation: there is no need to look any further, and it may not have any obvious bearing on your life. Or you can pay attention to any insights that occur to you during such an experience, and the consequences of such insights. The insights and understanding matter more than the quality of the experience itself.

I doubt if any human being can continuously observe that extraordinary experience of centreless freedom in every moment. I certainly have never met such a person. The mind moves in mindful and less-than-mindful ways. That does not deny this immeasurable freedom at the core of being, but it does make allowances for our humanity. The everyday mind has a place in the scheme of things, though in an awakened life it never has to stretch far from the centreless freedom that lies at the root of all things. The apple never falls far from the tree. In this centreless freedom there is no suffering, no dissatisfaction whatsoever.

There is a common misconception that if we were egoless, that profound moment wouldn't fade and would always stay with us. We would live our lives thoroughly clear and knowledgeable about everything and every issue. We would have insight into every area of interest to us. But it would be foolish to imagine that immeasurable freedom offers omniscience. This is an idealised version of liberation, not enjoyed by the Buddha or any teacher since. Out of the great depth of a liberating experience comes a knowledge of freedom in daily life. Such knowledge, grounded in awareness, makes it clear that freedom lies at the root of being.

We can easily assume that Dharma teachings point to liberation as an experience of absolute clarity about everything in every moment of existence. That would give us extraordinary power. We would be able to predict with absolute certainty the consequences of our actions. We would know everything that goes on in the past, present and future. There is no evidence that any human being has ever reached such a point.

Predictions about the future from prophets, religious texts and astrologers abound. We want to believe that certain people can look down the tunnel of time, perceive all the conditions available, and accurately state what will happen in the future.

When John the Baptist predicted the coming of the Messiah, Salome persuaded Herod to have the prophet's head cut off. When religious people and astrologers make predictions about the future, they too lose their heads. No one on earth has the absolute authority to predict the future with complete accuracy.

Yet, a timeless knowing is liberating and unstoppable. This knowing never concerns itself with the changing face of past, present and future. We can know freedom. We can know an awakened life, and know its presence in our existence. We can know the value of living a noble way of life. We can know the emptiness of the ego, and the emptiness of fixed views about cause and effect. We can know the emptiness of craving, clinging and possessiveness. We can know an end to suffering over this and that.

We can know happiness and deep contentment. We can know there is nowhere to go, nothing to get, and nothing worth getting caught up in. We can know the importance of treating others as we wish to be treated, and we can know the power of friendship. We can know the end of belief in birth and death. We can know the Deathless, we can know Nirvana. There is nothing more we need to know.

# THE EYE OF
# WISDOM

*In Eastern teachings, there are references to the Eye of Wisdom,
sometimes called the third eye. It sounds mystical, but it is a
beautiful way of describing the all-seeing nature of wisdom.*

A young woman felt the limitations of her daily life. The religion of
her upbringing had never appealed to her. Then she watched a
television documentary on Hinduism that fascinated her. She felt
that Western religions' attempts to dismiss Hinduism as simply
belief in hundreds of Gods said more about Western attitudes than
the deeper truths of Hinduism. She went off to her local bookshop
to read more. There were many concepts that seemed strange to
her – reincarnation, samsara, karma, Brahman, the third eye, and
so on. She knew that if she could probe into this somewhat bewil-
dering array of concepts, she might uncover some deeper truths.

I met the young woman when she turned up for a workshop I
gave in California on Buddhist teachings and insight meditation. In
Eastern teachings, there are references to the Eye of Wisdom,
sometimes called the third eye. It sounds mystical, but it is a beautiful way of describing the all-seeing nature of wisdom. When we
look around us through our ordinary eyes, we see a whole variety of
colours, forms and shapes. When our eyes are open, there is no
selection and rejection. Visible objects make contact with our eyes
as splashes of colour, and simultaneously we recognise through
perception what the colours represent. When we see the world of
colours and forms, we know our eyes are open.

Seeing through the Eye of Wisdom means seeing without the
intrusion of the ego, allowing everything to take place without discrimination. The Eye of Wisdom sees and knows things as they are.

Sights and sounds, feelings and thoughts all appear and disappear before it. It has no distinguishing mark or characteristics, nor can it be known as a thing in itself. It does not abide in time, place, or space. Its nature is pure peace, pure reality without limits.

The Eye of Wisdom opens through the choiceless witnessing of all that life entails. Ultimately, nothing obscures reality. The Eye of Wisdom remains forever open, revealing the emptiness of the ego and the notion of the problematic self caught in problematic circumstances.

This Eye of Wisdom is freedom. The pleasures and pains of daily life contain within them the 'I' that arises in conjunction with time, objects and experience: 'This happened to me', 'I had this experience'. The discovery of the Eye of Wisdom embraces all fields of experience equally. Presence and absence of experience make no difference to the true nature of things. Nothing has to happen to me to open the Eye. The Eye with which I see the Truth is the same Eye with which the Truth sees me. This Wisdom stands above all laws of conditionality.

The young woman spent more time meditating. She knew that the third eye mattered more than her two physical eyes. Of course, she knew that good eyesight matters enormously, in the conventional world, yet she now had another priority – to open the Third Eye. I reminded her that the Buddha said that to one who 'sees' the Truth clearly, it is as obvious as colour is to a person with good eyesight.

# THE MAYA
# OF TIME

*Teachings of liberation challenge us to realise the*
*Timeless, where we discover true fulfilment.*

The fact that things are by common consent thought to be a certain way is no evidence that they really are so, and it is important we make this very clear in our lives. This gives us some inner space from which to question, and to support our reservations about those who claim to be living in the real world. Obviously, we can't function in society unless we operate within conventional reality. However, Buddhist teachings and spiritual practices are not concerned with helping people to fit into conventional roles, but with getting to the heart of the matter.

We have a problem if we believe that the generally accepted view of existence is true reality. If we don't look beyond it, we are lost in a dream-world. Buddhists and Hindus have a name for this dream-world: Maya. Maya implies living in an illusion. It means believing in conventional realities as being ultimately the way things are. Dare we question this social conditioning and all the clever voices behind it?

For example, we can inquire into our notions of past, present and future. When we say, 'I am thinking about the future', what are we really talking about? Where is the future? It doesn't exist. It can't be shown or revealed. It can't be found anywhere. It is a product of thinking, simply a movement of the mind. There isn't something separate called 'the future' that we can think about.

Similarly, when we turn our attention to the past, there is an inner movement composed of feelings, thoughts and ideas that we call memory. We say we are remembering something that took place in the past as though that past event is something defined, separate and objective. We imagine we are going back to it in a factual way. However, we can't. We simply experience feelings, thoughts and ideas, with no past thing to take hold of. Dwelling in images gives us the belief that there is indeed some *thing* called 'the past' that is separate from everything else. There isn't. What we know all expresses itself in the here and now, whether mental or material. We cannot ever reach into the past. Even when we understand this, when we talk about the past or the future in our day-to-day life we have to use accepted, conventional ways of speaking. (The more accurate alternative would be to keep including 'as if' – *as if* there were a thing called future with an independent existence, *as if* there were an independent past that can be referred to.)

When we view past and future with awareness of their insubstantiality, it unpacks the solid constructions we have around issues involving time. If we don't unpack our fixed perceptions, we accept time as ultimately real (rather than an illusion), and believe everything belongs in time. Solidifying past and future into realities generates a fixed view of existence and makes us socially acceptable. And that's about all.

If we had enough interest, insight and depth of understanding, our problems associated with the past would disappear and become as unreal and fictional as the idea of the past is. Similarly, problems associated with the future would disappear if we could see through the idea of an independently existing future.

Where does that leave the present? Owing to the potency of our conditioning, we identify strongly with our feelings, thoughts, moods and perceptions. These become lost in today's events. Again, we easily give substance to the movements of mind that act like a shadow over the present moment. We then distort the present moment. We become locked in a fictional world of identity and roles that act like filters on our present experience. It is no wonder that we feel something is missing when we look into the field of time in this conditioned way. Living in time with our self caught up in past, present and future is inevitably unfulfilling, since ultimately this is not the way things truly are.

Teachings of liberation challenge us to realise the Timeless, where we discover true fulfilment. Work, daily life and our state of mind are all just things we put together and make something of.

Such activities arise and dissolve in the field of time and vice versa. They are simply combinations of circumstances. We must not be afraid to put them into that perspective.

Ultimately we must come to *know* the Timeless that makes all possible. That *knowing* reveals no form, colour, sound, smell, taste, thought, feeling, or ideas. The Buddhist tradition reminds us to see the emptiness of what we construct. This whole world of past, present and future; life and death; roles and activities all manifest out of a Timeless nature. All teachings, meditations and practices point to That. There is a contentment to this Timeless discovery that knows neither beginning nor end. We know fulfilment. We have come home.

# WHERE IS THE
# DIVINE?

*For some people, devotion to an external object which they
perceive as divine belongs to the path of spiritual practice.
However, it is easy to confuse the means with the end.*

The expression of devotion is common to almost all the world's
religions. In devotion, the heart responds to something greater than
itself. A relationship is established between the devotee and the
object of that devotion – often called God. However, a tremendous
gap remains between what is called 'the Divine' and ourselves.
This gap seems so large, and the Divine so distant from the self,
that something – a book, guru, incarnation, or whatever – is often
required to act as a link or bridge to the Divine.

For some devotees, this gap between the devotee and the object
of their devotion doesn't really matter, and they are genuinely content to love and serve God as a lifelong activity. Others love their
guru, or another link to the Divine, as a representation of something very profound and enlightening, not questioning why they
treat the guru as special and extraordinary while their perception of
others, including themselves, remains less than special. Other
devotees see themselves as a reflection of the Divine or a drop in the
ocean of the Divine. This helps them to feel less distant from the
Divine, since they are an expression of that which is Immeasurable.

There are other expressions of devotion equally, or perhaps
more, important: devotion to an ethical way of life; devotion to the
here and now; devotion to opening the heart; and devotion to a fully
awakened life. Is devotion to God the most noble expression of
awareness available to humanity? What about people who aren't
inspired to such devotion? What hope is there for those who can't

find fulfilment in churches, mosques and temples? Are holy texts, saints, priests, gurus, lamas and masters that important?

If we look for the Divine outside ourselves, we are looking in the wrong direction. To engage in worship of another, living or dead, embodied or formless, amounts to looking in the wrong direction for liberation. In this respect, churches, synagogues and temples at best act as reminders of the Divine. If we let go of the idea of worship, we can look at any expression that reveals the Divine within.

The Buddha taught the importance of the four kinds of Divine Abiding. He said when we express love and kindness, this is Divine. When we express compassion, this is Divine. When we express appreciative joy, this is Divine. When we express equanimity in the face of pleasure and pain, this is Divine. We do not need to create religious buildings, huge statues and institutions to experience the Divine. We need teachings and spiritual practices that enable us to access it. A divine way of life is found in the heart, not in submitting to beliefs. It requires tremendous devotion to keeping our hearts and minds well adjusted to the circumstances of daily life.

Even this reinterpretation of divinity is not the end of the journey. Sometimes we forget that Dharma teachings in their full potential are about closing the gap. They point to the utter completion of the entire evolutionary process. Even the beautiful and divine expressions of the heart are dependently arising and passing. How many times in our life have we shown acts of kindness that are temporary?

For some people, devotion to an external object which they perceive as divine belongs to the path of spiritual practice. However, it is easy to confuse the means with the end. There is something far more important than the sweet taste of love and devotion. What is That not tied to the deepest inner feelings of the Divine? What is That not tied up with religion or science? What is left when we put everything aside including all expressions of devotion? What is left when we have nothing and nobody to turn our attention to?

We may be left with a feeling of being nowhere and being nobody. We may have nothing left to rest or stand on. We have kicked away every crutch, every support for consciousness, and have discarded any lingering uncertainty. There is nothing left whatsoever. In this state, we may be very close to the truth of things. The truth of things stands steady, unlike matters of the heart that arise and pass.

It may be that such considerations never cross our mind. We may have put a lot of effort into living a good life, loved our neighbours and engaged in 'pujas' (acts of worship to our God). We consider, and rightly so, that all of this makes us better human beings. It also keeps our religious traditions alive. However, it would be a pity to refuse ourselves a chance to die to all this. It would be a pity not to take the opportunity to go to a wild and isolated place in order to experience nothing but the sky above and the earth below; to be naked in this world. It is only when we are stripped down to nothing that we have any hope of understanding what an awakened life means.

# WHAT IS
# FREEDOM?

*We can reflect on freedom, meditate on freedom and contemplate its significance. We can recall moments of great freedom and times when freedom seems far away.*

When we say that we live in the 'free world', we usually mean that we have political freedom, opportunities in life, the ability to grow materially and economically, and the freedom to pursue our own aims and interests. Just recently, I read an article about the resources available on this planet. All the tropical rainforests, minerals, oil and so on would be totally exhausted within five years if all the people in the world were brought up to a Western standard of living. The freedom that is bound up with individualism – the freedom to go and get what 'I' want within the framework of the law and social acceptability – is not sustainable on this planet. Our basic capital, namely the earth, cannot tolerate such a demand.

We also talk about another kind of freedom referred to as liberation, emancipation, or salvation in religious traditions. It is offered as the supreme prize in our existence and is described in all the different religions. Some teachers of salvation care little for the fragile state of the world. Others become so identified with their claims to enlightenment, to the experience of God in their life, that they make life intolerable for others.

When I reflect on this, something deep inside me whispers there is something unsatisfactory about indifference to the fate of the earth or claims to be the 'only way' to liberation. Something seems to be missing. There seems to be a lack of understanding about our natural intimacy with all of life. We can certainly regard freedom as the most important aspect of life, and secular and religious people feel attracted to freedom. But rather than identifying ourselves with one type or the other, we must ask ourselves, 'What does it mean to *me* to be a free human being? Free from what? Free to do what? Free despite what? Free in the face of what?'

There are many areas of life in which freedom is concerned – politics, financial matters, personal issues, family issues, religious beliefs, speech and language, social issues. Since it is such a core issue in human existence, it deserves our attention. We can reflect on freedom, meditate on freedom and contemplate its significance. We can recall moments of great freedom and times when freedom seems far away. We need to explore if anything inherently stops freedom, whether we are in a loveless marriage, in prison, or dealing with a life-threatening illness.

We need to re-evaluate what freedom means in light of how the world is today. Authentic liberation arises from the depth of our being, of our awareness and commitment to the plight of others and the earth. The lives of present and future generations have become vulnerable due to the force of desire and demands upon life.

We have to keep asking what it means to be a truly free human being. Freedom has often been thought of as personal salvation or as freedom for our particular group, but these viewpoints are exclusive and do not consider what it would mean to be personally free while simultaneously including the freedom of others. In light of the circumstances in which we live on this planet at this particular time, we must consider the freedom of all beings. Liberation cannot be thought of in exclusive terms. The freedom of one is vitally linked with the freedom of all. Our freedom must support the freedom of others.

# THE ARCHER

*If we are willing to look into our own state of consciousness, we
can see for ourselves what is appropriate. This is self-knowledge.*

There are three common types of experience. One is deep sleep;
the second is the dream-world; and the third is the waking state.
We find ourselves moving between all three, but the dream-world
and the waking state can mimic each other. A dream can seem like
reality until we wake up. In the same way, the waking state is a
dream-world when we spend our time wandering from one thing to
another and living in highs and lows. As in a dream, we imagine it
is reality. It is only when we truly wake up that we know the waking state is a dream-world as well.

How much effort should we apply to our journey to full awakening? To what extent should we try to develop concentration in
meditation in order to make something happen in our consciousness? Should we take a more laid-back attitude, settling in and
allowing things to unfold by themselves, or push toward the goal
we have set ourselves? Different teachers, books and traditions give
different answers. We must decide for ourselves which is preferable. How can someone else tell us what to do with our own minds?
If we are willing to look into our own state of consciousness, we can
see for ourselves what is appropriate. This is self-knowledge.

Finding wisdom in such circumstances is called 'the middle
way'. We learn to trust more in ourselves. When we depend on the
authority of others, it is at the expense of knowing ourselves. There
is no point trying to be a carbon copy of other people. Instead, we
can explore the resources available for enlightenment. We can put
our faith in what works for us at a particular time, and move on
when necessary. Nothing is worth clinging to. There is no point in
pushing ourselves too hard nor taking the easy route. We can trust

our inner being to awaken and re-awaken if we start sleepwalking through life again.

For some people, a settled approach without pushing the mind is appropriate. They bring their attention back when it wanders so that they remain quietly aware throughout the day. Developing an emphasis on sustained mindfulness throughout the day contributes significantly to a contented mind. However, there is a limitation to this approach if we live as though there is no further to go than that. Such mindful living is only a springboard to full awakening.

Another approach is one of concentration and hard discipline in meditation. Some Buddhist traditions adopt a tougher regime on retreats, including many hours of sitting utterly still to develop a concentrated mind. This works well for some practitioners and not for others. Little sleep, limited food and intensive practice offer a samurai quality to the path of enlightenment. Some people need that. Yet for others, this practice can generate tension and pressure by reinforcing the striving mind: they become very goal oriented. Natural wisdom will reveal the benefits and limitations for us of a particular practice.

There is a story of a person who went to Japan to study and practise archery. For months and months, the master archer of the school gave the pupil instructions on how to cut wood and make bows and arrows. Then the student learned correct posture and how to hold the bow. Then he learned how to pull back the string.

At first he had no strength and lacked the power to pull back the string even a little bit. Through diligence and practice, he learnt to pull the string back without tension or force. Then he found an easier way to hold the bow. He discovered that when he held the bow low, he could pull the string back more easily. One day the master saw him doing this and turned his back on the student saying, 'Ha, I can't teach you anything.' The student said, 'When I hold the bow high, my arm aches. This way is much easier.'

The master replied, 'I'm not here to teach you the easier way.' (Sometimes we need to be in an uncomfortable situation. We need to experience the unpleasant, to go out on the rough sea. Anyone can be a captain on a calm sea.) The archer continued to learn the rudiments of firing an arrow. After some years, the day came for him to fire his first arrow. Facing the target, he stood poised, pulled the arrow back and aimed at the target. Then the master said, 'No, not today.' The student could not understand why.

He had done five years of work in preparation for this day when he could fire his first arrow. Later, the master told him to prepare himself again to fire an arrow. As he was ready to let the string go, the master again said, 'Not today.' This happened several times. Finally, the student looked the master in the eye, broke out into a broad smile, took the bow and arrows and snapped them. He threw the pieces on the ground and walked away free. The student had woken up.

The master burst into laughter, bowed politely, and said, 'The teaching is over.' Finally, we have to stand on our own two feet, not just listen to the experts, even those with much wisdom. Then we can experience our freedom from dependency. Having woken up, we know the dream-world as a dream-world. We forget that our conditioned mind with all its personal ramifications belongs to maya, the world of illusion. The student expressed his independence to the master, and the master knew he had just witnessed freedom of expression, not a reckless impulse. The student had cast aside the bows and arrows of existence. The master bowed down to his student.

# LIFE IS A GIFT

*There is a sense of something quietly awesome that is equally*
*revealed in any movement of mind, any state of experience, and*
*any occurrence taking place.*

If we are honest with ourselves, we realise that we persistently view
the present as a means towards an end. According to conventional
reality, the events of the present moment are the result of causes in
the past. What we do with those results, how we react to them, in
turn sows the seeds of future effects. This is the world we live in.
We see causes in the past; experience the effects of them in the present; respond or react to these effects; and so convert them into new
causes of future events.

When we look at life this way, we are trapped. We don't really
see the world – all we see is how it is for *me*, what it means to *me*,
and what *I* have to get from it. In this way, the present is a com-
modity that we consume, manipulate and exploit; something we
can use now to profit from in the future. Even when we talk about
inner work – seeing clearly, inquiring, investigating and seeing into
things – our mind wants something from it. What would it mean to
look at life without asking anything from it – even if for only a
moment?

From another perspective, life is a gift, and the concept of a
separate, demanding self in relationship with everything else is
nothing more than a distorted idea. When we see in this way, we
cannot hold on to even one single experience. Whether or not the
'I' comes in and says 'this is me, this is mine', life keeps unfolding.
Whether we like it or not, want it or not, approve of it or not, it still
keeps emerging. It doesn't matter whether we interpret it as a
means to an end; life still keeps revealing itself and fading. This
unfolding keeps taking place according to its own nature. When we

are connected with this process, the 'I' doesn't really matter that much. Life isn't something to affirm *me*, nor something that *I* am going to control.

Are we willing to allow life to be a gift? Are we willing to regard whatever unfolds as an offering that makes the self seem almost irrelevant? When we view life with simple humility, without attributing it to any source or using any labels, we see that it is all a vast offering. You only have to look up at the night sky to see how immense it all is. You only have to focus your eyes on a sunrise, a flower or an insect making its way across the path to see this.

Untainted by thoughts of what we are going to get out of them, these direct perceptions touch upon what is vast. There is no concern with cause and effect, no means and ends, and no results. There is a sense of something quietly awesome that is equally revealed in any movement of mind, any state of experience, and any occurrence taking place. Whether the mind is dull, cloudy and confused; or bright and full of energy, it's all the same revelation. We couldn't have one without the other.

Life is an offering, a gift without measure. It is not a gift to individuals, but a presence available to any alert consciousness. If we can put aside our personal storyline, even for a few moments, we might touch upon something that goes beyond all measure. To do so could have an extraordinary impact upon our life. We could see through so many petty preoccupations when we have access to a different dimension.

Life is extraordinary because we can't ever get a handle on it. We can't get our mind around this experience of living. It is a wonderful thing to make the journey through life knowing fully what it means to live in an awakened state that no event can corrupt.

# ENLIGHTENMENT:
# NEAR OR FAR?

*We need to learn to stay with the truth of our experience,*
*whether we like it or not. The truth counts, so we practise this*
*until we know what it means to live with the truth of things.*

It is a noble commitment to work towards enlightenment. Even if
this concept is alien to our culture, there are more important issues
than cultural tendencies. For enlightenment, we must be willing to
step outside of the so-called norm and make our personal journey
into life. In the course of such a commitment, we often feel far from
enlightenment. This is especially true when we are struggling with
doubt. We try to get rid of our doubts, believing that once they are
behind us it will be plain sailing. In doubt, there is a duality. 'Shall
I continue or shall I discontinue?' 'Is this worthwhile or isn't it?'
'Will things improve or will they stay the same?'

Such doubts are not as meaningful as they appear. To change
our way of looking at them requires experimentation, reflection and
learning to accommodate. If we push our doubts away, we might
lose a valuable opportunity. When we recognise a dual state of
mind about whether to do this or that, we have the opportunity in
meditation to pierce this bubble of confusion, to see the emptiness
of it. Knowing the bare truth of states of mind places us in the
region of enlightenment, but it may not feel like that – it is important not to rely upon our feelings to measure how close we are to
enlightenment.

It's generally understood that one function of meditation is to
reduce doubts so that our mind is not constantly moving backwards
and forwards between so-called choices or options. We carry with
us the idea that living with truth ought to be agreeable, but it may

not be. The truth is that our mind may be in a state of doubt and we are finding things hard to resolve. At such a time, this is the truth of our experience. We need to learn to stay with the truth of our experience, whether we like it or not. The truth counts, so we practise this until we know what it means to live with the truth of things.

When we are steady with the truth of things, we will know the benefit. It is the truth that counts, not trying to make our experiences fit into a view that says we should be happy in every moment. The truth stays steady in the face of doubts that emerge unexpectedly from within. None of what goes on in the mind or body makes a difference to the truth; any experience confirms the truth as much as any other experience.

There is no greater challenge than to know the truth and live with it. This is true whether we experience dilemmas or utter harmony of perceptions. The sun shines regardless of the number of clouds that pass by.

# FIT TO RECEIVE

*To be fit to receive affects every facet of your life, every area of
your existence. When you realise this, you are no longer living in
a tiny restricted corner of your mind.*

It is important to remember that a step back from something
reveals a corresponding step towards something else. Meditation,
reflection, service and mindful living act as the catalysts for discovery. Finding inner well-being allows us to step back even from
calmness of mind.

It is standing back that makes you fit to receive. Only in this
position of receptivity can we speak of being in a state of innocence.
There is no wish to reach out to anything, let alone a desire to reach
out and harm anyone. This innocence has nothing to do with a
childlike mentality: it is a purity of consciousness in which there is
a state of unknowing, and you abide in receptivity.

You may wonder, 'Is there anything I can do?' but there is
nothing you can do. There is nowhere to go. The idea of gaining
something and getting somewhere becomes crude. Consciousness
is in a state of inner repose. Then deeper intimations begin to be
expressed. They begin to draw our consciousness towards enlightened understanding. We are drawn in an inner direction without
making any effort. No effort, no matter how willing and well motivated, needs to be present. For if it were present, it would distort
the innocence by creating a goal, a desirable end. For consciousness
to evolve, it must go without an act of will, and must find its own
course. Its journey travels from the known to the unknown.

There is a natural inner movement towards touching something profound. We are like a magnet – drawn inexorably towards
that which is beyond comprehension. There is a connection
between consciousness and the pure intimation of something else

205

altogether. In addition, of course, in this inner journey thought has long been left behind. In this inner movement, consciousness itself opens up; and the innocence begins to manifest as clarity and insight. Access to such depths is unavailable through will-power and thoughts. To be fit to receive affects every facet of your life; every area of your existence. When you realise this, you are no longer living in a tiny restricted corner of your mind. Events cannot buffet what is mysterious and incomprehensible.

Yet we are human. There are times when we lose access to such deep discoveries. When you experience the richness of inner life, you access what is vast. You know where your consciousness is at different times. You know the relativity of what is happening to you psychologically, physically, mentally and spiritually. In such depths, consciousness embraces it all.

This seeing expands both inwardly and outwardly. What was previously unknown becomes known, moves to the foreground of consciousness, and is seen clearly. Love, joy and insight are intimations of enlightenment. In the unknown, in that beautiful state of innocence, there is a mystery. Words and formulations can never explain this mystery, and can never be converted into something that is familiar.

This mystery can never lose its awesome flavour or its capacity for enlightening our life. That is not possible. In being with this mystery, or even being close to it, consciousness itself undergoes change. The relationship between consciousness and mystery is cemented through love and realisation. You are an expression of that mystery. In the depth of being, there is a blessedness revealing everything. Just everything.

For further information about retreats offering Dharma teachings
and Insight Meditation, please write to:

Insight Meditation Society
1230 Pleasant Street
Barre, MA 01005
(978) 355-4378

Spirit Rock Meditation Center
P.O. Box 909
5000 Sir Francis Drake Blvd.
Woodacre, CA 94973
(415) 488-0164

Gaia House Trust
West Ogwell
near Newton Abbot
near Newton Abbot
Devon TQ9 6EN
England
tel: 44 (0) 1626 333613
fax: 44 (0) 1626 352650
e-mail: gaiahouse@gn.apc.org
World Wide Web Pages:
www.gn.apc.org/gaiahouse
www.insightmeditation.org

# About the Author

Christopher Titmuss is the co-founder of one of the largest and most respected retreat centres in Devon, from where he travels all over the world to teach awakening and insight meditation retreats. From 1962 to 1969 he worked as a reporter in London, Turkey, Thailand, Laos and Australia – and then spent six years as a Buddhist monk in Thailand and India. For the last twenty-five years he has been teaching the Dharma. He is an active supporter of global responsibility and is a founder member of the 12-strong international board of the Buddhist Peace Fellowship. In 1986 and 1992 he stood for Parliament for the Green Party.